The Signs of God

The Signs of God

First published in the United States in 2001 by
The Golden Sufi Center
P.O. Box 428, Inverness, California 94937.

Printed and bound by Thomson-Shore, Inc.

Library of Congress Cataloging-in-Publication Data

Vaughan-Lee, Llewellyn
    The signs of God / by Llewellyn Vaughan-Lee.
       p. cm.
    Includes bibliographical references and index.
    ISBN 1-890350-04-4 (pbk. : alk. paper)
    1. Spiritual life. I. Title

    BL624.V386 2001
    297.4'4--dc21   00-068149

CONTENTS

～

We will show them our signs on the horizons
and in themselves.

(Qur'an 41:53)

～

PREFACE

Throughout this book, in an effort to maintain continuity and simplicity of text, God, the Great Beloved, is referred to as He. Of course, the Absolute Truth is neither masculine nor feminine. As much as It has a divine masculine side, so It has an awe-inspiring feminine aspect.

Lover and Beloved

Man is my secret and I am his secret.
The inner knowledge of the spiritual essence
is a secret of my secrets.

hadîth

THE SECRET SUBSTANCE OF DIVINE LOVE

The mystical relationship of lover and Beloved is one of mankind's greatest secrets. It embraces all of creation and yet takes place within the human heart. The soul's love affair with God is a passion that transforms the whole human being and reveals the hidden face of the world. The mystical journey is an unfolding of this love affair, a giving of oneself to God through love. Because this love belongs to oneness, it takes us back to oneness. The wayfarer is brought home from a life of separation to an experience of being merged into Him.

This journey is only possible because of a substance within the heart, which the Sufis call *sirr*. Without this substance there would be no journey and no spiritual awareness, no knowledge of union. *Sirr* is a gift of God to those who love Him, and is given for the sake of realizing the truth and then being in service to truth. *Sirr* means secret and belongs to the mystery of divine love, of the relationship of lover and Beloved that takes place within the innermost chamber of the heart, the heart of hearts as it is called by the Sufis. This substance is the secret of the universe and the essence of His love for us. Hidden from the world because it does not belong to the world, *sirr* reveals to us the essential oneness of our relationship with Him.

Much of the work of the path is a process of preparation, an inner purification to enable the heart of the
lover to contain His secret without its being contaminated by the ego or lower nature, the *nafs*. When the
disciple is ready, then the *sirr* is given from heart to heart,
usually through the presence of a living master, a *sat
guru*. This substance of divine love is infused into the
heart of the lover and activated by divine love. In the
words of the tenth-century mystic al-Hakîm at-Tirmidhî:

> Within the heart God placed the Knowledge of Him
> and He lit it with the Divine Light.... By this light
> He gave the heart eyes to see.[1]

The secret substance within the heart is the organ
of divine consciousness, a consciousness of the oneness
of God. A mystic is one who is able to bear this secret, to
live His oneness. The path prepares us, but His gift is
always an act of grace, given with love by love. And it
brings with it the responsibilities of the heart, to be in
service and to live according to the ways of love and not
the ways of the mind or the ego. Love demands that we
sacrifice ourself, because, in the words of the great lover
al-Hallâj, "When truth has taken hold of a heart she
empties it of all but herself."

In order for His secret to be infused into our heart
we have to give our heart to God. Then our heart is "held
between the two fingers of God, and He turns it as He
wills." A mystic is someone who is born to do this work,
"who was intoxicated by wine before the creation of the
vine." Before we are born we are branded by love; we
come into the world to be of service to love. Often unknowingly, we are taken into the arena of love, where we
are asked to sacrifice ourselves. The blood of our heart,
the tears of our soul are our pledge to love. Our duty is to

keep alive the connection within the heart, so that His secret can work within ourself and within the world.

LIVING HIS LOVE

To be a lover of God is to be drawn into the mystery of love, into the unfolding essential unity that is hidden within the heart. This love that is given as a gift is born into consciousness with the tears of separation, with the longing that breaks open the heart. Love awakens us with the call of the reed that is torn from the reed bed, the anguish of the soul that comes to know that it is separate from its Beloved. The eleventh-century Sufi Abû Sa'id ibn Abî-l-Khayr said, "Sufism was at first heartache. Only later it became something to talk about." To be a Sufi is to live this cry of the soul, this primal pain of separation. Longing takes us back to love, and the price is tears stained with the blood of the heart.

The journey of the lover is a one-way street of love, and our tears carry us into an abyss of longing, of aloneness and anguish. But in this desert of desolation when despair seems our only company, something is born, something infinitely precious and tender beyond our understanding. Our soul senses the intimacy of its Beloved, that He is as close as "the tears that run between the eye and the eye-lid." We begin to experience a love affair that is as intoxicating as it is painful, as wondrous as it is terrifying. We are awakened to the softness of His touch, to the sweetness of His embrace.

These are the secrets of the mystic, of one who has been taken by love. For each lover this love affair is unique and often too intimate to be told. It is what we have always wanted, what gives our life its real meaning. Whether in the sweetness of His touch or the intense pain of being without our Beloved, we are caught in the grip of a love that consumes our whole being. The love and longing awakened within the heart are all that is real. In the moments of sweetness and of pain we know that we are connected to our Beloved. We feel the value of our heart's sorrow, and know how precious is this thread of longing.

The mystical path is living the connection of the heart, the innermost connection of love. We aspire to remain with Him, to keep our attention on our Beloved. We long to be with Him whom we love; we need to see the face of our Beloved. And yet the world distracts us, and so easily we seem to lose our connection. We are caught in the affairs of the world, in our daily desires and problems. How quickly do we forget our heart's true desire! The veils of the world close tightly around us, seducing us with its myriad images. And then suddenly our heart calls to us and again we remember. We turn back to Him to whom we belong. We are reawakened to love.

And so we make our gradual journey back to love, our spiraling path that takes us deeper and deeper within. He whom we love is always with us, whispering the secrets of love; and we need Him and yet forget Him. And in the midst of our heart, hidden even from our knowing, the mystery of divine love begins to reveal itself. In our heart of hearts the grace of God changes the substance of our being. Gradually we are permeated from within by a light that belongs to the sun of suns, by a love that is pure presence. "It takes time to make a soul pregnant with God," but this is the miracle that is being born within us.

Why are some chosen to live this life of love-longing? Because it is His will, because in the tapestry of His creation He has made some human beings to live the life of His lover. They are "branded by God" and can belong to no other. No other relationship will fulfill them; no human lover can take hold of their heart. They can fall in love with a human partner, but something is always missing, an essential note cannot be played. However much outer life seems to offer, only one thing really matters: the heart's love affair with God.

It is not easy to belong to God. He is a jealous lover and demands our complete attention. We give our whole life and our heart for the purpose of love. Pledged to love, we are emptied of everything that might interfere with the work of love. We are remade as a mirror for the love of God so that it can shine into His world. We are polished by our problems, by the difficulties of our life, and the pain of our love for our Beloved.

The work of the lover is to be attentive to love, to stay with the inner connection of the heart despite all of life's difficulties, despite the distractions that surround us. We cry, we pray, we fight to remain looking towards our Beloved. We strive to keep our heart clean. We work upon ourself diligently, with perseverance and patience. With the practices of the path, meditation, the *dhikr* (the repetition of the name of God), we aspire to remember Him with each and every breath. We live the fullness of our outer life, family and work, and at the same time struggle to keep our inner attention focused on the heart. For the one thing that really matters, that absorbs our inner attention, is the demand of our love for Him and His need for us.

THE REMEMBRANCE OF LOVE

Love embraces us and love tears us apart. Love is a knife that cuts us and a softness that kills us. We are taken away from ourself and given to our Beloved. We are given back to the oneness of love, His oneness that is stamped within the heart. How this happens cannot be known to the mind. It is too deep a secret. The life of the mystic is to live this secret, to live a giving of oneself that is complete and absolute, until nothing remains of the lover but a shell, an outer covering in which love can unfold its purpose. In the words of Majnun:

> Love is the essence of my being. Love is fire and I am wood burnt by the flame. Love has moved in and adorned the house, my Self tied up its bundle and left. You imagine that you see me, but I no longer exist: what remains is the Beloved.[2]

The mystery of lover and Beloved is hidden within the heart of every soul that is seeking God. His love is the thread that guides us back to Him, and our sorrow is the sweetness of our remembrance. And yet as a culture we have almost forgotten this love. As we wait on the borders of a new age there is a great need to remind ourself of our real nature, of the oneness that embraces every cell of our body and every sigh of our soul. We need to reclaim the sanctity of mystical love and make it conscious, to bring this ancient secret into the marketplace of our world.

His lovers are here for this purpose. They have come together from across millennia to awaken the world to its innermost connection of love. What is lived within their own heart belongs to humanity; it is an essential part of the mystery of mankind. Without this thread of divine love the song of the world would be lost, the music that gives meaning to our ordinary life would fade away.

And yet we stand on the edge of an abyss of forget-fulness. Caught up in consumerism, blinded by greed and rationalism, we have almost cut the thread of our soul's devotion. We are lost to such a degree that we hardly even know that we are lost. We have forgotten our real nature and the sacredness of all that is created. We think that we are here for our own purpose, and have forgotten that the world belongs to God.

Mystical love has an essential purity because it looks only to God. It is awakened as a memory of when we were together with our Beloved, and His lover longs to return to this state. Mystical love cannot be caught in the de-sires of the ego or the patterns that imprison us. His love is too free; its fire burns too hot. Mystical love reminds us of that which is pure and unpolluted, of that which is sacred and sings the name of God. Mystical love opens a doorway through which His grace can flow into this world. The essential oneness of lover and Beloved re-minds us of what we have almost forgotten, that there is nothing other than God.

"He loves them and they love Him." (Qur'an 5:59) His lovers are born to live this mystery and bring it into the world. When their hearts cry to God His song is heard. When they melt in His embrace His love is felt. When the memory of the heart is awakened creation comes to know to whom it belongs. In the silence of our sorrow we know Him. In the bliss of union we celebrate His oneness. And the heart of His lover gives this secret of creation back to the world:

> And in everything there is a witness for Him
> that points to the fact that He is One.

Living the Moment of the Soul

But listen to me: for one moment,
quit being sad. Hear blessings
dropping their blossoms
around you. God.

Rûmî[1]

THE LINK OF LOVE

The secret of the mystical journey is that in the core of every human heart is a connection of love that directly links lover and Beloved. When God looks into the heart of those who belong to Him, this divine link is activated. It is in this moment that the journey begins, that the attention of the lover is drawn back to the source, and the lover begins to seek her Beloved.

The awakening of the heart, the activation of this secret link of love, is an act of grace, given because He wills. The work of the seeker, of the one who is drawn on the mystical journey, is to live this link of love. This journey calls to us, and leads us away from the attractions of the world to the deeper attraction of our heart's Beloved. The destiny of the mystic is to be awakened to this relationship of love, to live a life of longing, to live, fully, the life of a lover who seeks only her Beloved, and, ultimately, to be drawn by this longing into the mystery of union. The mystic must prepare for love's call, and live this strangest of love affairs amidst all of the contradictions and pressures of the world.

All of creation belongs to God and witnesses Him: every atom praises its Lord. This is the deepest song of creation, without which the world would fall apart. But only some human beings are called to make this work conscious, to know the secret face of creation. The hearts of those who are drawn into the arena of divine love are imprinted with a bond between lover and Beloved. This imprint is a part of the destiny of the soul and marks those who belong to Him. The purpose of the mystic's life is to live this belonging, until with every breath she feels the innermost link of love that runs between the worlds. Then the lover holds the two worlds united in her heart, and knows the secret of divine oneness.

PURIFICATION

For those interested in spiritual life, worldly challenges hold little interest. Instead, they are called to use their gift of consciousness to praise and honor Him who gave them this gift, whose divine spark they carry within their heart. In order to praise Him more fully, to worship Him more completely, these individuals are drawn into religious or spiritual lives. Through the teachings and practices of the path, through prayer and devotion, they are able to purify themselves so that they can worship Him more deeply, so that their spiritual aspirations can become less obstructed by worldly desires or by instinctual drives. The work of purification helps us become more accessible to His will and His love, so that we can listen more attentively to His voice and be more sensitive to His guidance.

Much of religious or spiritual life is a process of purification, whether this is done through exercise, chanting, fasting, or prayer. The more the practitioner works upon herself, the more she has access to her spiritual nature, the part of her that looks towards God. Gradually more and more of her consciousness becomes accessible to spiritual purposes; she is able to use more of this divine gift for its higher purpose: to praise and witness Him. This work is a lifetime's struggle, a continuing process of purification, and the individual is constantly challenged by conflicting feelings and thoughts, by the desires of the ego and the pull of her own lower nature, what the Sufis call the *nafs*.

Today much of the process of purification takes the form of psychological work: confronting and integrating the shadow and other conflicting aspects of our psyche. Finding our faults is not just a process of separating the light from the dark, but also of integrating our darkness. For each of us it means taking upon ourselves the responsibility of being human. As we are taken into the realm of our own complexities, the price of self-knowledge is always more responsibility. We have to become responsible for our own darkness, for our own pain and lack of self-worth.

Slowly, gradually, the effort is rewarded; light is found in the darkness and it becomes easier and easier to look towards God. The religious or spiritual life becomes all-embracing as the individual is drawn more completely into the circle of remembrance. Then His love shines more directly into our lives; the path of the soul is more visible. Those who remember God look towards Him and come to know how much they are loved and supported in all aspects of their lives, in every moment of their day.

Purification is an essential aspect of spiritual life and religious life. Yet one of the distinguishing features of this work of preparation is that it remains focused on the transformation of the seeker herself. Progressing through predominantly linear and often predictable stages, the process of purification brings the seeker along the spiritual path towards the goals specific to her spiritual system. Much of contemporary spirituality that centers on personal development and transformation uses models of purification as the basis of its approach. It is here that real mysticism is distinguished from spirituality, as the mystical journey is never about the mystic.

THERE IS NO DERVISH...

For the lover of God purification is only preparation, part of the work that takes us to the arena of love. The real mystical journey is what happens when we lose ourselves, when we become absorbed in God. Within the circle of His love there is no path and no wayfarer, just a deepening absorption, a dissolving into what cannot be named. Here, the mystical truth that "there is no dervish, or if there is a dervish that dervish is not there" becomes a lived reality.

The mystical journey belongs to love, and not to any practices of purification. Having drunk the wine of divine intoxication "before the creation of the vine," the mystic is born into this circle of love. She carries its hidden imprint as a scar within the heart. For the mystic there is neither the safety of a journey of spiritual ascent nor the certainty of redemption; there is neither paradise nor purgatory. The lover of God is not interested in personal salvation or enlightenment. Rather, she is destined to live a passion that has no boundaries, only the all-consuming nature of divine love.

That the mystical journey is not about the wayfarer, or leads to the death of the wayfarer, is so alien to our culture of self-identification as to be almost incomprehensible. Consequently, mysticism is generally misunderstood in the West. Even contemporary spiritual traditions more often than not confuse the work of preparation and purification with real mysticism. Spiritual traditions that have flourished in the West have simply given Western values of individuality and progress a spiritual twist. Replacing material with spiritual well-being has placed spirituality firmly within our collective horizon. We have been given a spiritual rather than material dream to pursue. This may have made spirituality more accessible to a Western culture, but has done nothing to support a true mystical orientation.

Our culture is so addicted to achievement, to progress, and the siren of success, that we seem unable to escape this fantasy. We imagine that spiritual practices and techniques will free us from the limitations of our ego-self, not realizing that the images of progress and goals that we project onto our new-found spiritual stage belong to the ego. No longer focusing on a better material life, we aspire towards spiritual goals, not realizing that we have just recreated a different form of self-interest. Is the enlightenment or inner peace we seek fundamentally different from the American dream of prosperity? Are we not just becoming slaves to another god or demon, another illusion? Sadly we do not recognize how easily we can lose the thread of our soul's devotion in the mirage of conditioned spirituality.

How can we reclaim mysticism from the clutter and confusion of our contemporary spiritual marketplace? How can we discern the true freedom of our soul, the freedom in which everything is given, from the promises and practices of personal liberation? The mystic who has given herself to love knows what is beyond the borders of culture and conditioning. She inhabits a region of the soul where love and service are given freely and there is neither striving nor achievement. Living a relationship of oneness, she recognizes that the deepest longing of her heart belongs not to herself but to her Beloved.

Those who belong to this "brotherhood of migrants who keep watch on the world and for the world" live without leaving traces, and are usually unrecognizable. In the outer world they are part of the crowd, playing their part, indistinguishable and unnoticed. Yet they hold the keys to the inner world, to the dimension of the soul and the real freedom that belongs to love. Belonging neither to this world nor to the next, they are the servants of love and carry the wisdom that comes from a commitment to love.

Unattached to form or structure, His lovers flow with the need of the time, wear the clothing and follow the outer customs of their environment. But inwardly they belong only to love, and are the guardians of the ways of love. Since the beginning of time they have played their part in the world, keeping open the gates of love and ensuring that His grace flows freely into His world. Because they belong only to their Beloved, and seek neither material nor spiritual gain, they can do this work. Empty of intention, they are a part of the will and ways of their Beloved.

There is a need for the ways of love to be reclaimed and made conscious, for the hidden ways of devotion and mystical belonging to be made known. In their simplicity and ordinariness those who belong to God have remained hidden, enabling them to pursue their work of devotion and remembrance without interference. But underneath our present collective clamoring for spirituality there is a hunger for what is Real; there is a longing for pathways unpolluted by the conditioning of self-interest. His lovers hold the keys of these pathways in their heart, and can read the signs that lead seekers to the truth.

THE MOMENT OF THE SOUL

We live in a time when many of us are desperate for spiritual sustenance. We long for a love that penetrates us beyond repair, that demands our most sincere attention, that draws us always more deeply into life and connects us more fully with who we truly are. We want to live a relationship with unlimited love and boundless freedom. But is our collective spirituality too firmly set in its ways of self-improvement, in its goals and objectives, to listen to the simple cries of the heart that carry one beyond time and space, beyond gain and loss? Can it separate out the limitless and formless truth from the constricting influences of contemporary culture? In the circle of divine love there are few signposts and no progress. As a Sufi saint replied to a question about spiritual progress, "Swimming in the infinite ocean, who is nearer the shore?" Giving up any sense of self-advancement and personal involvement, the wayfarer surrenders to the truth that "Allâh guides to Allâh whom Allâh will."

God's lovers belong only to love; thus they are unconstrained by personal or cultural conditioning. As such, they embody a deep and powerful freedom that can profoundly affect the destiny of the world. Mystics have a part to play in its present unfolding and there is a call for their mysteries to be made known and enter the collective consciousness of our time. The secrets of divine love carry the fragrance of the future, a future born from the eternal moment of the soul.

Only too often we recreate our future out of the patterns of our past, and so remain imprisoned and unchanged. With the best of intentions we seek change, not realizing the depths of our conditioning, how much it influences our thought-patterns and behavior. The tools we bring to free us from our limitations carry the imprint of our forefathers, and so only vary the design of our imprisonment. Seeking freedom, we are naively hopeful, not realizing that we create our future in the mirror of our past.

Yet there are moments when something breaks through that does not belong to our conditioning. There are instances when the clouds part and there is a glimpse of real sunlight, as T.S. Eliot describes:

> Dry the pool, dry concrete, brown edged,
> And the pool was filled with water out of sunlight,
> And the lotus rose, quietly, quietly,
> The surface glittered out of heart of light....
> Then a cloud passed and the pool was empty.[2]

Sometimes these "moments in and out of time" belong to our personal life. These are moments when a door is opened for us so we might enter a reality beyond our normal experience. In these moments we are given the opportunity to access qualities and experiences of the soul that are most often obscured by our mental or psychological habits and needs. We might be overwhelmed by the joy that is the essence of life, feel the love that creates life, or sense the oneness that is the root of life. We might hear the music of our own soul, or rest in the eternal silence of pure being. Or we might be struck with awe and wonder as we look upon creation as though for the first time. Like the memory of a summer kiss, almost forgotten, or the scent of an evening storm just approaching, these moments slice through time and present us with something as complete as it is unending. These mystical experiences are given to us with grace, and they can come in the silence of nature, in the presence of great art or beauty, or in any moment that touches us. We sense something deeper than ourselves—in the words of the poet Wordsworth,

> a sense sublime
> Of something far more deeply interfused,
> Whose dwelling is the light of setting suns.[3]

Why are we given these moments? It is the grace of God and a reminder of our real nature. From these moments real change is possible, because they carry an energy that is unconditioned and belongs neither to ourselves nor to our environment. These moments vibrate at a higher frequency than the mind, and so they penetrate beyond our mental and psychological limitations. They can awaken us to a reality that is not distorted by fears or caught in the grip of ego-dynamics. It is up to us how we use these moments. They can alter our life, or just serve as a reminder of a reality beyond our understanding. We can dismiss or cherish them, learn to be always attentive to their possible return, or live in regret that we appear to be banished from this paradise shown to us.

Many people remember a wonder that was present for a few years of childhood. This is a natural state that some people seem to be given. Often this early wonder is accompanied by the experience of being close to God, of an unlearned relationship with their true Friend, a closeness without conflict or the distortions of personality. That He is present is so natural that nothing is said. Years later these memories can surface with a quality of amazement that then it was so easy and natural.

Often in adolescence we experience similar moments in which we step into a world free from cultural and personal conditioning. We can be shown the real possibility of life, its potency and splendor. We may be given the image of an ideal which we long to live, even to fight for. But sadly, these moments and what they bring to us are only too quickly lost; they dissolve like a dream as the "realities" of adult life take hold. Maybe such moments will return; something eternal will reach for us like a lost love. Then once again for an instant a doorway reappears and life is present in a way we could never have imagined.

If we let them, these moments can nourish us in a way nothing else can. They feed us with the eternal substance of our own soul, with something unpolluted, unconstricted, and eternally beautiful. For just a moment they awaken us, before they "fade into the light of common day." Later they may come in times of great need, even despair, when something within us cries out, when there is a primal need to feel the meaning of our life. As mystics we allow these moments to take and transform us, to remind us of our true nature and the abundance of His oneness.

These moments do not belong to us and do not arise from our psychological patterns or our past. Like the sunlight they are free and speak of freedom. And like all true gifts, we cannot possess them. They are precious beyond our comprehension, and their purity protects them from being constrained by our own experiences or desires. We can discard them or just watch as they fade away, but because they do not belong to us we cannot destroy them by trying to fit them into our own conceptual frameworks. We can forget or remember them, discount or honor them, but their essence remains always imprinted into our soul like a scent, or a memory.

THE CHILD OF THE MOMENT

The Sufi is known as "the child of the moment" because she learns how to live in the eternal moment of the soul.

Her work of purification is to be an empty cup into which the grace of her Beloved can be poured. Her practice of inner attention is to be receptive to the need of the moment. The path takes her out of her limited self so that she can be a servant of the moment, a slave of the One she loves. The lover lives for the moment of His presence, just as she perseveres through the endless emptiness of His absence. But it is in the eternal moment made present that she becomes fully alive, responding from deep within to the call of her Lord.

The mystic belongs to this moment, knowing that although often hidden, it is present in each breath we take. The eternal moment is outside of time, is not a part of our past or our future, and yet it is to be lived amidst all of our everyday activities. His lovers have accepted the responsibility to be always attentive to the moment while pursuing their everyday activities. Mystics aspire to live the moment of His presence with the intensity and passion of a lover and with the receptivity of one who is always attentive to the needs of her Beloved.

It is in the eternal moment that love is born and the magic of life happens. Love does not belong to time, and its timeless quality is well known to all lovers. Love is experienced solely in the moment, and only too easily the mind with its patterns of past and future cuts through love's subtle substance, destroying its fragrance with doubts and arguments. Thus the lover has to learn to still the mind in order to catch the moment and stay true to love's unfolding. Then life begins to reveal its secret face, the magic of its deeper meaning: the eternal face of the Beloved becomes visible in His myriad forms.

Wayfarers tread a path that leads from the illusion of time to the eternal moment that belongs to the soul. In the midst of their daily activities they learn to stand outside of time and witness the way life evolves, the way situations form, coalesce, then dissolve or become fixed. Their practices free them from the limitations of a linear consciousness and they become inwardly attuned to the vertical dimension of their inner connection to love. They are trained to grasp the essence of a moment before it becomes defined and immutable, and they learn to live in the moment in a state of unconditioned freedom. Being in the world and yet not of the world, His lovers follow the ways of love and not the constricted patterns of cause and effect. They are able to stand alone and live the heart's inner connection regardless of the pressures of the outside world.

THE DOORS OF REMEMBRANCE

The heart's connection does not belong to time but is the thin thread that connects the two worlds, the world of the soul and the unfolding outer world of temporal events. This connection carries the essence of life, the love that is the seed of all becoming. Through this connection life reveals its real nature, the stamp of its creator. As outer life evolves in time, different aspects of the Creator are revealed. Evolution as we know it is a process of revelation in which He reveals Himself to Himself; or, as experienced within the heart, He reveals Himself to those who love Him. We are so conditioned as a culture to focus upon our own progress that we think that evolution is about us, the evolution of humanity. Thus we fail to grasp the deeper significance that evolution is about Him of whom the world is a reflection. Our collective blindness to this simple reality stops us from understanding the significant changes that are happening around us. Caught within our own hubris, we face the possibility of losing the meaning of this moment.

For the first time in millennia we live in a culture which is focused upon humanity rather than the divine. In the West we have forgotten the primal truth that the world belongs to God. We fail to acknowledge that everything happens according to His will and is a reflection of His oneness. As a result we remain stranded within the limited framework of our own consciousness. Seeing life only from a human perspective, a perspective dominated by our own needs and wants, we fail to grasp the larger picture that life has always presented to humanity. We fail to see the interrelationship of the human and the divine that is at play in every moment, and which gives color and real meaning to our lives.

Our culture is obsessed with its patterns of power, with its domination over the natural world and its progress in science. Christianity and the pursuit of rationalism banished God to the heavens and science has given us the illusion of control over the physical world. Like children we have played with the toys of our seeming success, with our material abundance. Gradually we have forgotten the real purpose of life, that we are here to praise and worship Him. We have become so addicted to our notions of progress that we have not realized that something essential is missing, that the colors have faded away and our life has become a blur of activity without joy or meaning. In essence we celebrate ourselves and not our Creator. We celebrate an illusory self rather than Him of whom all life is born and to whom all life returns.

How can we now reclaim our connection to the essence of life? How can we redeem a culture caught in such a pattern of hubris and forgetfulness? The mystic knows and lives the simple and yet revolutionary truth that everything happens according to His will. It is His will that we forgot Him, and if it is His will we will remember Him. The mystic also knows that as much as we had a part to play in His forgetfulness of Himself, so we have a part to play in His remembrance of Himself. The wayfarer who lives a commitment to love knows that lover and Beloved are one, and we carry His consciousness into His world; in the words of a Sufi saying, "We are the eyes and ears of God." His lovers know that if it is His will the doors of remembrance will open, not just within the heart of the individual seeker, but also within our collective consciousness. There will be the possibility of change that does not belong to the linear patterns of time, that does not belong to our self-centered dreams of a future of more material abundance.

Those who are drawn inward to where the soul is starved see something more essential emerging. They experience a collective howl of anguish as the psyche of man is battered by his addiction to external progress. And deeper than this despair they glimpse a hope that contains the seeds of a future uncontaminated by the excesses of the past—a future born out of a knowing of the sacred wholeness of life rather than the sense of individual isolation that we have created for ourselves.

Those who dare to live this hope within themselves will find that the hope connects them by an almost invisible web of light to others. This web of light is always present within humanity. It forms the human container of love and light that balances the darkness of our desires. This web of light is supported by devotion and prayer, without which real meaning would be almost unobtainable, love inaccessible, hope abandoned. The work of the lovers of God is to keep this web of light alive for humanity. This is the work they have been doing silently for centuries. They are the keepers of grace, creating an invisible support for what is most precious in this world.

This web of light forms part of the hidden structure of the world. In different times and different places it shines more brightly, is more visible. This is in accordance with the need of the time, the place, and the people. Through the hearts of His servants the light guides those who need, provides invisible love and support, and upholds the possibility for real change, not only to the individual but also to the whole of humanity. When humanity is in real need, then the servants of God work together to bring the light of His love as close to consciousness as is possible, without having its power unbalance the delicate structure of human consciousness.

This is a time of tremendous need and possibility for real change, a change that comes from within, from what is born anew within the heart and soul. But in order to grasp the real potential of this change one must separate oneself from the patterns of the collective. Just as in order to realize real change within oneself one has to be free of one's own conditioning, from the influence of one's family and past, so do we need to stand alone, apart from the collective, while in the midst of the present global crisis. Only when we stand alone and look within can we see our own radiance and its contribution to the web of light.

When we are alone we can see how we are held by the light of His love, are contained by the power of His presence. In our aloneness we can grasp the significance of the moment; we can realize its true potential for change. And yet we are always frightened to stand alone. We long for outer support and affirmation. We easily fall back into the patterns of the collective, and so sell the uniqueness of our own soul for a sense of security and belonging. And thus we lose the possibility for change and pawn our spiritual potential. We need to find the courage and commitment to stay true to what we have been given, to what is imprinted within our own heart. As Rûmî writes:

Don't be satisfied with stories, how things
have gone with others. Unfold
your own myth, without complicated explanation,
so everyone will understand the passage,
We have opened you.[4]

Just as there are moments of grace in the life of an
individual, moments "in and out of time" when we are
given a taste of a different way of being, so are there such
moments in our collective destiny. There are times in
the cycle of the planet when His grace opens a doorway
between the two worlds, when we are given the possibility to collectively incarnate a new quality of the divine.
These moments often come at a time of great need, as if
evoked by a collective despair, and they carry a seed of
divine hope, a hope in which everything is given. What
matters is that we live it, grasp the moment that is given,
and incarnate the seed of the future. Otherwise, we will
miss another opportunity and continue in our cycle of
self-destruction.

We are presently being offered such a moment, which
accounts for the flowering of spirituality in the West as
well as a new potential for global awareness, even global
responsibility. How we use this moment will affect the
course of the next millennium. Will we allow this influx
of grace to realize its real potential, or will we remain
caught within our collective values, seeking only personal profit and gain, material or spiritual? Will we create a space for what is being given, which means to step
into the unknown and undefined, or are we too imprisoned within our ways to notice the dawn?

A RETURN TO LOVE

In times of uncertainty, in moments of possibility, it is wise to return to what is essential. What is more essential than the link of love that is held within the heart? Love is what gives real substance to our lives, and yet it does not belong to us. Love belongs only to love and to the Lord of love. Love always points us in the direction of truth, and contains within it the seeds of our own unfolding. Love is the mystery of life, and we hunger for it, need it, embrace it, and run from it. Love calls us always towards greater possibilities, towards the flowering of our own soul and to the giving of ourselves to God. And love also gives meaning to the small moments of our day, as we remember the look of our child or the touch of our lover.

We know the importance of love, and yet we have forgotten that the heart holds the secret not just of sweetness and tenderness, but also of our individual and collective destiny. As the organ of divine consciousness, the heart is what connects us directly to our Lord, what links the lover to her Beloved. If we are to live the moment that is being given, if we are to step into the future that is already present, we need to reclaim the primacy of the heart and the wisdom and power of love. We need to return to the fundamental core of our own existence and know what it is that we are being offered. If enough of His lovers can do this work, then His grace can flow into the world and dissolve the patterns of collective conditioning that blind us to our real future. Then we can be open to receive what we have already been given.

Spiritual Responsibility

The first step is to cease isolating yourself from God.

Al-Hallâj

TURNING TOWARDS GOD

We are here for His sake. We turn towards God because He calls us, and the whole of our spiritual journey is an uncovering of His love for us. But how can we make this turn towards Him and live for Him when our whole sense of existence is focused upon our self? How can we learn to live His life, allow the Beloved to live His life within us? And how can we reconcile this with the responsibilities of everyday existence, the pressures and demands that continually confront us?

Mysticism is not an escape from the responsibilities and pressures of life. The Sufi master Bhai Sahib described mystical life as "to bear the heat and burden of the day." We have to learn to live the life of the soul, which itself is embodied in this world of form. The life of the soul embraces the two worlds, the outer dimension of time and space and the timelessness of the eternal moment. As a mystic you stand with "both feet firmly on the ground and with your head you support the sky." This is why mystical life is so demanding and why it is only for responsible men and women.

Becoming a responsible adult in our culture in this time of history is not easy. Not many of us are blessed with the inner stability a secure and loving childhood might provide us, which could enable us to stand on our own feet and make responsible decisions without outer help or guidance. And at the same time life has become increasingly complex, bombarding us with ever more information, opportunities, promises of fulfillment from a bewildering, endlessly expanding array of sources. We are expected to take our life in our hands and make the right choices, to make a success of it all, and yet we are given little guidance through this complex maze of possibilities, and few tools to deal with the confusions and insecurities and indecision that arise as we try to make our way. We easily become lost in the images and promises that surround and distort us, unable to find or live what is true to us.

Added to the extraordinary demands of growing up in this culture today is the fundamental spiritual disorientation experienced either consciously or unconsciously by so many of us. How can we know what we want from the world when we have lost touch with our real self? How can we be responsible for our own life and know our deepest needs when we have such a tenuous connection with our essential nature? Are we really living our own life, or merely the lives and fantasies of others, our parents, the images of our culture? And finally, how can we take real responsibility for our life if we do not know how to look towards Him to whom our life belongs?

THE COURAGE TO BE LOST

For many of us there comes a time when there seems to be no way forward, no way that echoes what we value or aspire to. This is the moment when we need to step aside from the stream of the collective, when we need to allow ourselves to become confused and lost.

For those who have the courage to become lost, a silent metamorphosis begins to take place. While our conditioned values tell us we need to know where we are going, the wayfarer begins to walk a different path—one that leads away from form and definitions towards the undefined and unexplored. If we step with both feet into this space of not knowing, a real hope can then surface. This is not the hope of a better future, not the hope born in patterns of time, but a hope that belongs to the rhythm of the soul, to the real becoming of ourself.

At this time those who want to make the journey leave behind the shore, while others stay close to the land, within the seeming security of the known. This is when mystical life becomes a lived possibility, when we can make the transition from a tangible world to one based upon the intangible sweetness of His love for us. For each of us this moment of transition will be different, and yet underneath it is the same because we are turning from our life to His life. We begin the great adventure, the search for what is real amidst the illusions of the world.

Taking this step is frightening. The wayfarer must leave behind everything she knows about her world. The sense of abandonment and loneliness can be overwhelming, and one must be strong and determined. But once you have seen through the collective bargaining of life, the mad rush of buying and selling that we have come to call progress, then a different picture can form. As in Plato's story of the cave, you step away from the shadows falling on the wall, and see beyond the entrance of the cave to where sunlight is reflected on the water. Then you can know the real laughter and joy of being alive for His sake. In this moment something else is born, a quality of being and becoming that belongs to the soul.

If we base our life and sense of purpose upon the ego, then we will be left with the shifting shadows of its illusory self. This is one of the oldest philosophical truths that has been engraved into the foundation of so many cultures before our own. The ego is an illusion and so its perception of life, its values and goals, are based upon an illusion. Yet today we have become experts at building upon this sand, forgetting the primal truth of the flow of the tide, and the storms that build up out at sea, the unexpected hurricanes that wash everything away.

Those who have the courage to lose what others consider precious can leave behind these shifting foundations. They can step into the hinterland of their own soul, and begin to take responsibility for what is really theirs. The responsibility of the soul takes us where we can never imagine, into both terror and beauty. And it allows us to reclaim what our culture has lost, the wonder of what it means to belong to God.

TAKING RESPONSIBILITY FOR ONE'S LIFE

To be responsible is to take your life in your hands and own your own power and purpose. It is to say "yes" to what you truly are, even though you do not yet know who you are. This is why it is a gamble that many avoid, preferring instead to live the safety of what is known and defined. To live oneself is always to step into the unknown: this is the adventure and the challenge. In the words of the Sufi master Abû Sa'îd:

> What you have in your mind, forget it. What you have in your hand, give it. And that which is to be your fate, face it.

Empty and unknowing, we can face the real adventure of life without the preconceptions that safely cover us. Naked and vulnerable, we cry from the depths of ourselves for something real. We embrace the eternal drama of being human, of being separate and alone. Only then can we see that our separation reflects His presence. Only then can we realize that we are here for His sake, realize it not as an abstract possibility, but as a lived experience. Then the cells of our body come to know Him and the passion of our soul lives Him.

When we say "yes" to our life we are faced with a tremendous challenge. We are faced with the pressures of the collective and their prescribed patterns. And when we decide to live our life for His sake, to incarnate our divinity, we are attacked by the darkness of our culture's collective denial, by the underlying anger that pervades our materialistic emptiness. Few seekers realize that they will have to confront not only their own pain, but also the collective curse of our material success. It is difficult enough to take responsibility for one's own personal dark-ness; how much more so to walk into the shadow-lands of our Western world. And yet we cannot avoid it.

Our personal destiny is bound together with our collective destiny, and to be true to oneself is to take one's place on the stage of the world. Freedom from the collective does not mean to escape or to withdraw, as I was once told in a dream: "The desert and mountains are no longer sacred places." We have to live our life where we are placed, where life has determined we are needed. This does not mean to avoid the possibility of choice or change, but to accept that we have a responsibility to-wards life, not only to ourself.

Just as personal transformation only happens through accepting one's own pain and darkness, so we need to take responsibility for what the collective rejects. We need to embrace our collective denial of His oneness, of the sacred nature of every breath we take. It is not enough to just re-establish a conscious connection to what is sacred. This is like redeeming our darkness by trying to be good. The darkness is then just covered over rather than transformed.

Unfortunately much contemporary spirituality, while well intentioned, does not address this basic psychological truth. For a while the spiritual energy appears to prevail, but there is little lasting transformation. In order to undergo real personal and collective spiritual transformation, we cannot simply turn towards the light; we need to take responsibility for the monster we have created, for the spiritual agony of our generation. And what the mystic knows is that only in the darkness of His apparent absence can His presence be rediscovered, only through the pain of separation can we make the journey Home.

The mystic neither seeks nor avoids suffering, is not bound by the pull of opposites. The mystic has made friends with her own darkness, with the sorrow of her own soul and the pain of the collective as well. The mystic knows that "everything is sweet if you taste it with care" and thus seeks neither salvation nor paradise. We do not try to escape from the present or create a better world. We know that only through living in the moment and bearing the heat and burden of the day is His oneness revealed, His presence made manifest. Because we belong to our Beloved, we accept both His light and His darkness, both the sweetness of His presence and the sorrow of His absence. Longing for neither this world nor the next, we know in our heart that everything is as He wills.

Through meditation and daily practice the mystic takes the power of His love into the darkness of a world that has forgotten Him. We know that we are here for His sake and so take full responsibility for our own incarnation. We live the pain of what the world has repressed, and thus bring this pain into the light of His love, into the arena of our own devotion. And we bear what we bear for His sake, and so avoid the patterns of ego-gratification that so easily subvert spiritual work.

BORN IN THE DARKNESS

The transformation of the shadow requires us first to consciously acknowledge what has been repressed and denied, and then to accept and integrate this shadow dynamic and its associated feelings. This requires us to work with any pain or guilt or other difficult feelings that might surface. Only then can the energy contained in the shadow be released, its power and potential be fully realized. The personal shadow contains not only negative qualities, but also unlived positive qualities, for example creativity or even a generosity that was not allowed in one's childhood. The same is true of the collective shadow. Our repressed anger and violence are well known, but have we discovered our denied devotion, our unlived love of God?

Working in the unconscious, we become familiar with that which is hidden. We find buried treasures, beauty, and horror. We also come to own and honor that which has been rejected and abused. Here, in the darkness of our contemporary world, there is a sacred wholeness that has been discarded by rationalism, a sense of wonder and a symbolic understanding of life. And deeper than this is the inner connection of the mystic, a direct access to the divine that so frightened the patriarchs of orthodox religion that through persecution and power they tried to eradicate it. How many mystics have been crucified, burned, or stoned to death? How much love has been lost to the world?

Mystics are those who belong to God and bow down before no other authority. They are destined to live this inner connection regardless of the pressures of the outer world, at the sacrifice of their own self. The very unconditional nature of their love and devotion is what makes them so dangerous to the power of the collective. And yet in their love is a quality of real freedom that is so valuable, essential in its uncompromising nature.

Spiritual freedom is dangerous and powerful. In *The Brothers Karamazov* Dostoyevsky tells the moving story of how Christ returns unannounced at the time of the Inquisition. He appears quietly, inconspicuously, but everyone recognizes him, drawn as if by an irresistible force. He walks among the people in silence, and the sun of love burns in his heart, stirring their hearts with responsive love.

But then the Grand Inquisitor appears and commands his guards to seize the man. They drag him to a dungeon, where the Grand Inquisitor confronts him: Fifteen centuries ago, the Inquisitor acknowledges, Christ brought freedom. But people do not want real freedom—they are too weak, worthless, vicious, and rebellious. The masses do not want bread from heaven, but earthly bread. So the church has vanquished freedom in order to make men happy. Tomorrow Christ will have to be burned at the stake as a heretic.

Christ is silent. His presence is freedom. Even if he is burned the freedom remains. Mystical truth may be denied, rejected, considered unnecessary. But its reality remains.

His lovers carry this truth, this essential freedom of love. They know that although the masses may not want this truth, may be too frightened by real freedom, it is still essential. For centuries they have kept this truth hidden, an esoteric secret taught to initiates, given with the different practices of devotion that belong to different groups of lovers, different orders of dervishes. His lovers are needed to live this freedom, to claim what the world has rejected. They are points of light unafraid of the darkness, because they know the deeper truth that everything belongs to God. They have made the journey into the darkness of their own souls and found that His love is present. They know the hope that is found only at the core of despair, the wonder that is revealed in the anguish of their own isolation. They have cried the tears of separation from God and known that it is His tears that stream down their face. Belonging neither to this world nor to the next, they carry the hope that is needed, and a love that is uncontaminated by personal need.

At times of possible collective change this freedom needs to be made known. The claims of the Grand Inquisitor need to be put to one side, and the secret of mystical love needs to become public. When the patterns of collective consciousness become so constricted that the light of the soul is obscured, then there is a danger to humanity. When the soul cannot breathe, cannot sing the praises of God because the collective thought-forms are so dense, we lose contact with our own center. As Yeats said,

> Turning and turning in the widening gyre
> the falcon cannot hear the falconer;
> Things fall apart, the center cannot hold;
> Mere anarchy is loosed upon the world.

When the love that is at the core of creation becomes obscured, when "the falcon cannot hear the falconer," then the soul of the world cries out, and those in service to love respond. This is when in the darkness of our denial of God something new and unknown can be born. Yeats knew that this was "The Second Coming":

> And what rough beast, its hour come at last,
> Slouches towards Bethlehem to be born?

Though we may not realize it, it is the "rough beast" that brings redemption and rebirth. That which has been rejected and discarded, hidden in the shadows of our success, is our salvation. Our own instinctual knowledge of God, our natural way to praise and love Him need to be reclaimed. We need to rediscover the sacred oneness that embraces all of life and knows the meaning of love and freedom.

BEING RESPONSIBLE FOR LOVE

What is it that we have lost? What is it that needs to be rediscovered, reclaimed, reborn? There is a love that is at the core of creation, a love that is born of oneness and carries the sacred interrelationship of all life. This love is alive within the heart of those who love Him; its music is the song of the soul and the hidden purpose of creation. There is a wonder in this love, as well as a terror and beauty. Its wonder and terror come from its unconstricted nature, its limitless freedom; its beauty is a reflection of the face of God.

But why do we avoid this love, the love that is hidden within our soul? Why do we avoid our own deepest destiny, our promise to live the life of the soul? There are so many apparent reasons: our fear, our desires, our laziness, our longing for security... The ego covers the soul with a myriad of excuses. To own His love is a painful business, a work born of a commitment to sacrifice, an honoring of that which has been rejected and despised. To take responsibility for the work of the soul—to live the destiny of a lover—is to walk into the fire.

When I lived in the same house as my teacher I was awed by the intensity of a life that is lived for His sake. My teacher lived with the totality of His demand and met it with the uncompromising nature that is needed to carry the call of love and respond to its needs. She was always attentive to a love that was both intoxicating and exhausting, a love that demanded complete sacrifice and service. Whoever came to her door with a need for love was given to, without any restriction, with the freedom that belongs to His love.

To honor the ways of love is not for the weak-hearted. A love that carries the sacred oneness of life belongs to life, and the real nature of life is unrestricted. The life that is present in each moment, the life that sings His praise, requires us to be awake and alert. Within the heart there are not the boundaries of time and space, and this is how we need to live. This is the inner attitude we carry as we walk in the world.

When we say "yes" to His love we accept the responsibility of a life that does not belong to ourself. Our life may often seem to reflect the ordinary pattern of home and work, but this is only an appearance. Beneath the surface we are not allowed to live attentive only to our needs. We are trained to avoid following the pull of our desires, the desires that focus on ourselves. Instead we work to leave a space for love in each moment of our day. Most of this work is inward, reflecting the hidden, invisible nature of love.

AN OPPORTUNITY FOR FREEDOM

All of creation exists for His sake, and yet our culture has forgotten this. Addicted to our own progress, to the illusions we have created, we have come to believe that we are here for our own sake, that life is in service to us. We see our fleeting presence upon the stage of life as an end in itself, not recognizing the most fundamental aspect of our existence. This is like a wheel without a hub, an orchestra without a conductor, a day without sun.

Is it arrogance or ignorance that has brought us here, that has left us spinning without a center? Can we recognize what we have lost, surrender our claims to self-importance? The present moment is full of opportunity, opportunity to reclaim our real self and awaken a consciousness that contains the sacred oneness of life. Yet many powerful forces are holding us back. These forces belong to that which is established, patterns that have power over us. They influence our actions, and more important, they color the quality of our thinking. They prevent freedom and spiritual devotion from entering into our spectrum of consciousness.

These forces are very powerful, and have been built up over centuries. They are the vested interests of our culture, those that have most to lose by real change. Working on the level of the mind, they influence our thought-patterns and choices. Looking to the outer world we can easily see the visible vested interests of our culture, its global companies, political organizations. But because of our culture's dismissal of the inner world, we fail to recognize the power of collective thought-forms, of the mental attitudes that influence all of us. The Grand Inquisitor still denies us our spiritual freedom, imprisons and then destroys the heretical consciousness of pure love. Our mental patterns instead promote self-interest and greed. We are pressured to consume the "earthly bread" and are denied access to "bread from heaven." How easy it is to think that money or possessions will bring you fulfillment. Does this thought belong to you? Where did it come from? Do we realize how strong a collective thought-form is?

The potency of love is that it does not confront a collective thought-form, nor does it impose its own ideology. Love has a quality of freedom that neither constricts nor confronts. Love allows what is natural within us to be born into consciousness. Love takes us by the hand and shows us the doorway through which shines the sunlight of our true nature, and love gives us the choice to walk through. If we choose to remain in the darkness of material greed, our ego-oriented values, love does not reject us nor does it forget us. Love "bears all things" and "endures all things." Love allows us to live according to our own choosing. Love just offers us the possibility for freedom, the possibility to follow the thread of our soul's destiny. It is for us to take responsibility for how we wish to live.

His lovers work to remind the world that it has the possibility to return to love. They open the door to the sunlight of the beyond and keep alive the hope within the heart. They have given themselves to this work, and are bound in freedom for His sake. At this moment in time they are needed to subtly infiltrate the thought-forms of the collective with the possibility of a life that is not bound by greed or the power structures of the present. Like a mirror their hearts and minds reflect a light that cannot be filtered out by the control mechanisms that distort so much of our present perception. They do not try to change the world, because that would mean to be caught within the chains of desire. But their hearts carry a love that goes where it is needed. And this love is infused with a quality of consciousness that the world needs. Empty of intent, they look towards their Beloved. But the look of His lover sings of selfless devotion. It is an affirmation of the heart's knowledge of God and how the world reflects His oneness. As a friend was told in a dream, "We don't try to change the color of the sky. We just love God."

THE SEED OF THE FUTURE

Mystical love and the knowledge of this love are a seed for the future, a seed for a possible spiritual reawakening in which the sanctity of life is included within a direct perception of the oneness of God. The monotheistic religions celebrated His oneness, proclaimed that there is no other God than He. But the price of this religious evolution was the sanctity of all that is created. As the many gods of ancient life gave way to one God, a sacred and richly symbolic world, in which each stream and tree was an embodied spirit, was lost. The tapestry of divine manifestation and the symbolic relationship of each part to the whole were replaced by the primacy of man and his relationship to one God who exists outside of creation.

As divine immanence became overshadowed by His transcendence, mankind slowly lost touch with the oneness that is present within creation. This world was no longer understood as a manifestation of the hidden face of God, but rather as a place of separation before our return to paradise. As the oneness of God became banished from our world, mankind came to regard itself as the ruler of the planet. Patriarchal consciousness imposed its power structures, and this world ceased to be a place of revelation. Gradually we abandoned our quest for the signs of God that are hidden in every shape and form, although poets and artists have tried to remind us of this wonder.

At each moment of time the creation reflects an aspect of its Creator. And human beings have the potential to consciously live this, to know that they are a part of the wonder of the way the world reflects God. Halfway between heaven and earth, human beings belong to both the manifest and what is hidden. They are a doorway between the two worlds and thus have the potential to have revealed to them the secret of the word *Kun!* (Be).

Through the heart's innermost connection to the divine, and the stream of love that flows along this connection, the secret of life and love can come into the world. Within the heart the unmanifest and the manifest aspects of the divine unite. If it is His will this union can give birth to the child of the future, a child whose eyes are stars and who knows the meaning of the names of God.

When life is consciously lived for His sake, the doorway between the worlds opens and grace flows into the world. This grace is needed for the birth of the child of the future. Without this grace the world will remain sterile, a wasteland without opportunity. His lovers are working to create an opportunity for a union of light and dark, what is visible and what is hidden, the masculine and feminine. In their hearts they know the hidden essence of their Beloved. In their life they see His face made visible, His names made manifest. They carry the knowing of what can be born from this union, and offer it to Him to whom they belong.

We wait, attentive to our Beloved. We know that we are in His hands, and yet we need to live the responsibility of our devotion. The sorrow of our separation from our Beloved has given us hope, the darkness of our despair has given us light, our longing has taken us back to our Beloved. What the lover discovers through her pain is the eternal presence of her Beloved. What is lost is always present; He can never forget us. But we need to accept the pain of our collective forgetfulness, of our culture's separation from God. We need to know that we turned away, and that if it is His will we can turn back to Him, and the sanctity of life can be redeemed. The child of the future is our own offering to life. It is our life lived for His sake.

The Power of
Forgetfulness

If you can penetrate the center of time and space,
You can bypass the addictions of the world.

Shabistarî[1]

BANISHED FROM PARADISE

Why do we deny His presence? Why do we turn our
attention away from our Lord and back to ourself? Why
do we reject one of the greatest mysteries of being
human, that we are made in the image of God? We
have been driven out of paradise, exiled from a state of
oneness with Him, and rather than confront the pain of
our banishment we have turned away from God and
immersed ourself in forgetfulness.

Forgetfulness is woven into the fabric of the world's
illusions. The desires, attractions, and discords of His
world cover our eyes. "Lead us not into temptation,"
implores the Lord's Prayer, and an essential aspect of the
world's temptation is the drug of forgetfulness, the sleep
in which we forget our real nature and Him to whom we
belong. We each have our own way of hiding from the
truth; we keep the curtains closed lest the dawn awaken
us. Each day we try to shield ourselves from the haunting
desolation of a world without Him.

We busy ourself in life, not realizing how much we
are driven by the myth of what we have lost. Our deep
need to be absorbed into oneness enacts itself in our
addictions, and in the way we try to lose ourself in work
or relationships. We ache for something real, yet we settle

for what is most convenient—a Hollywood adventure, a more powerful computer, our latest romance—while somewhere we know these will never satisfy us. Our fantasies tell the real story, a longing to reclaim something, to find the perfect partner, to know that we are loved completely. Exile is a strange world of half-truths. The signposts are everywhere, and yet we overlook them again and again.

Forgetfulness itself is an addiction, a drug so powerful that we become our own jailers. We have used the consciousness that could free us to create a world that denies Him. We delight in our success, in our vision of progress. We have created a strange world of excesses and hunger, of technology and human emptiness. Plagued by a vague sense of something missing, we invent and produce in a desperate attempt to bring to life something that will fulfill us. Yet we do not dare to acknowledge what we have forgotten.

We have based a whole civilization on the myth of forgetfulness, on the image of a world that does not honor its Creator. We justify our lives with so many illusions. In the West we even proclaim the ideal of freedom. And yet we have forgotten the most fundamental freedom of being human, that we can turn towards God. We have forgotten the freedom of our real self, of what is deepest within the human being, the freedom of unconditional love.

We have the potential to remember our Lord, to rediscover His presence. But this would mean consciously confronting the pain of separation, the agony of our exile. Those who love God have paid the price of remembrance, are awake to the sorrow of separation. They carry the consciousness of love—a bright light that can break through the murky haze that covers our culture. They can remind the world of the possibility of real freedom.

THE POWER OF THE COLLECTIVE

We must not underestimate the pull of forgetfulness. The fog which covers our perception is a very real presence on the inner planes, and is held in place by structures of power created and maintained by the collective. Our collective conditioning forms the basis of our relationship to life and society and encompasses our patterns of behavior and our value systems. It provides us with its well-defined goals and images of success. The collective creates the thought-forms that determine our vision of life, and their influence is far more powerful and pervasive than we generally recognize.

To confront the collective and cut through the fog of forgetfulness is dangerous and demanding, as the pressures of denial are very powerful. The collective is threatened by the solitary soul who can see through its web of coercion. The individual who tries to break free challenges the collective, which tries to reclaim this individual by evoking guilt, shame, doubts, or other unconscious fears and anxieties.

In previous eras the pull of the collective was necessary for physical survival. The tribe could only survive as a whole. Anyone claiming individual freedom was a threat, and was shamed back into the collective. We have evolved beyond simple tribal life and its physical constrictions; America is a very mobile culture, and the individual can easily move away from his family or "tribe." But the psychological patterns of the collective are more difficult to leave behind, because they are imprinted into our unconscious. Anyone who has tried to become free from social patterns of conditioning and live true to her own inner self, knows how hard it is to escape the imprint of the collective, just as it is difficult to become free of an inner parent figure. Rebellion is just being caught in the shadow-dynamic of the social structure. Real freedom is bought with the pain of aloneness, a price few are prepared to pay. Only fools and those close to God dare to claim their birthright, which has been given to humanity.

LOVE'S PROTECTION

A spiritual path gives us practices to strengthen us and often a community to support us as we work to counter the unconscious forces that would deny us our freedom. A spiritual group is of tremendous importance in providing a container that can protect us against the negative influence of the collective, particularly the feelings of isolation and alienation that so easily attack us.[2] The support of a group can also help overcome feelings of shame and other undermining emotions that can surface as we journey beneath the covering that protects the collective from the raw energies of the archetypal world.

A group supports us; a path protects us with the invisible presence of all those who have gone before us. Our spiritual ancestors are with us, helping us, sustaining us. The friends of God, whether in this world or the next, give silent support to all those who seek the freedom of devotional love, who want to give themselves to God.

Devotional love itself has the power to align us with what is real. The heart that looks towards God is infused with His grace, with the light of His love. This light can break through the patterns of conditioning within both the individual and the collective. His love is freedom and allows us to live His freedom. Through the power of love we can glimpse what is real and bring it into our life, despite the pervasiveness of the collective.

As we surrender to God He gives us what we need. The more we surrender, the more completely we are given to. We may have to fight for the freedom to surrender, to give ourself to love, but once we have claimed the honesty of our convictions, the depth of our need, then we can give ourself more easily. The very act of opening the door of our longing and offering ourself to God breaks the power of the collective with its primal grip of self-interest and survival. If we give ourself to God we do not need the collective, nor are we focused on our own well-being. The servant looks towards his master and is only attentive to His needs.

When we make the simple turn towards God we consciously place ourself under the protection of our Beloved. Those who are blind to the values of this world are embraced by His light, a light that has power to protect and brightness to dispel the antagonism of the collective. The work of the lover is to stay true to this inner core of pure love, and so remain under the light of His protection. If we lose this orientation and stray back to our insecurities and defenses, then we come under the influence of other forces of the collective. Denial seeps into our psyche through our doubts and engulfs us without our knowing what is happening.

It is so easy to lose what we have been given, to fall back into the shadow-land of self-doubt and other feelings and thoughts that undermine us. What we do not realize is how much these negative patterns are influenced by the collective. We can often recognize their origin in our family dynamics, but the influence of the collective is less clear. The boundaries between our personal and collective psyche are very vague and the collective shadow permeates our personal shadow more than we are aware. Falling back from the clear light of our innermost connection onto the shifting sands of the ego, we are continually undermined by the flow of collective forces.

STRUGGLING AGAINST THE COLLECTIVE

It is so easy to become lost, to wander down the by-ways of collective thought-forms, to get caught in their dramas. In our culture there are few temples to retreat to, few ashrams to protect us against the world. We have to live our longing from within society, not isolated from it. And yet as we continue on the path we become more open, more sensitive to external forces. As the identity with the ego begins to dissolve, there is an added danger of identifying with what does not belong to oneself.

The collective can come in and take hold in many ways, slipping in through our weaknesses and inattentiveness, often filling a space that, for our inner integrity, needs to be kept empty. To hold an empty space of inner attention is more demanding than we realize. Our culture conditions us to fill what is empty, to turn away from the attentiveness of inaction into the busyness of activity. Thought-forms color the air with bright and seductive images, drawing us away from our real self and capturing our attention in the wonder of *maya*.

The collective has forces at its disposal more powerful than we are aware. We may have banished dragons along with other monsters and myths, but their existence is still very real. The archetypes, the gods of old, pull us through the cracks in our social values, where we have become weak and vulnerable, and one may become unknowingly sucked into a powerful unconscious dynamic that on the surface appears trivial. Is a continual desire for new clothes an aspect of self-expression, an enjoyment of beauty, or has our conditioning convinced us of our physical imperfection and lack of self-worth, drawing us into a narcissistic obsession with our self-image? Do television systems with sixty stations satisfy our need for variety and opportunity, or are we being caught in a strange aberration of the god of communication, offering us so many diversions that we forget what really interests us? Mercury is the messenger of the gods, but we have lost this all-important aspect of his work, denied our link with the gods. Instead we are becoming addicted to more and more forms of communication—from e-mail to cell phones—that paradoxically often isolate us from real human contact.

We do not understand the power of these archetypal forces, which far exceed any "personal" demons. Nor do we recognize what is happening when what may seem like a straightforward need or interest becomes an opening for these forces to take hold of us. In the archetypal world we quicky lose the power of discrimination and become unable to distinguish what is a real need from a distracting desire. And the seeker who aspires to live in an ascetic world of denial is no less vulnerable; repressing her desires, she may force them to act out their attraction through unwanted fantasies or obsessions. Ancient civilizations had good reason to placate the gods with sacrifices. Such rituals recognized the power of the archetypes. Our culture's denial of the archetypal realm has given greater power and influence to these primal forces. Just as the rejection of the personal shadow increases its destructive potential, our ignorance and dismissal of archetypal energies have a dangerous effect. Anyone who journeys in search of her true individuality will have to encounter these forces, will feel the pull of the collective with its thought-forms and desires, its subversive attacks of guilt or self-doubt. And the aloneness of the mystical journey can at times make us very susceptible to being drawn back into the collective. Yet present psychology, which has begun to map our personal psyche, has little understanding of the deeper, collective or archetypal realms and its inhabitants. Claiming our own freedom is still a heroic quest, with the added difficulty that we are not forewarned as to the monsters of the deep—we do not even know of their existence.

Often we succumb to the pull of the collective, and to the deeper allure of returning to the primal oneness of the unconscious world. Unknowingly we indulge the longing to lose ourself and the burden of our individuality. The pull of the Great Mother, the desire to return to her arms, is very potent, and she arouses in us a sense of paradise that is blissful because it is unconscious.[3] The energy of the collective seduces us with this promise of unconsciousness, of forgetfulness and merging, and with no longer having to fight to claim our real self. This may appear very similar to spiritual surrender or other mystical states, but is quite different—our individual self is lost in the unconscious rather than consciously offered to our Beloved. If we resist the pull of the collective we will realize that what awaits us is something much more beautiful and powerful: to live in the space of our own aloneness, a simplicity of being in which everything is present.

Mystical consciousness carries a responsibility to stay with one's essential nature and not be caught in distractions or unconscious dynamics. Only when we stay true to our self can we claim the thin thread that connects the worlds. Holding this thread, being attentive to love, requires diligence and devotion, and is a full-time activity. And yet we are surrounded by the clamor of so much activity and so many multi-colored distractions, physical, mental, and psychological. We are seduced again and again by personal weaknesses, external influences, and unconscious forces. And the effect of these forces is greater if we do not know them. We may recognize some of the "demons" that distract us, but the unconscious is the mistress of illusion and metamorphosis, and often we are taken unaware.

HIS REMEMBRANCE OF US

"He loves them and they love Him" is stamped into the core of our being, yet to live the simplicity of this love affair requires a perseverance tested in the fires of detachment. The Beloved is jealous and demanding, and we have to live with commitment and attention to stay within the circle of His love. But when He opens the eye of our heart we are able to catch the joy and wonder of His moment that is always present:

> Sudden in a shaft of sunlight
> Even while the dust moves
> There rises the hidden laughter
> Of children in the foliage
> Quick now, here, now, always—
> Ridiculous the waste sad time
> Stretching before and after.[4]

We carry within us knowledge of our own freedom. We may have been barred from paradise but we know that there is, in the midst of this world, a state of completeness, a moment in which everything is present. We sense the waste of a life that does not catch this light, that is lost in doubts and anxieties. And so we work on ourself, aspire, struggle with the tools we have been given. Yet often the fog of our collective forgetfulness keeps us isolated within our own effort. We know only our own endeavor, and it can feel so inadequate, fragile, easily dispersed.

Remembrance expels forgetfulness. But more potent than our remembrance of Him is His remembrance of us. His remembrance of us precedes our remembrance of Him, as the great Sufi Bâyezîd Bistâmî came to realize:

> At the beginning I was mistaken in four respects. I concerned myself to remember God, to know Him, to love Him and to seek Him. When I had come to the end I saw that He had remembered me before I remembered Him, that His knowledge of me had preceded my knowledge of Him, that His love towards me had existed before my love to Him and He had sought me before I sought Him.[5]

Isolated within our own self, we are denied access to the power of His remembrance. But when we turn towards Him we move into the vortex of His love and His remembrance. His remembrance of us is like a clear bell that resonates within us, dispelling the darkness of our despair, the sorrow of our aloneness. Suddenly we find that we are no longer alone; a softness enters our heart, a joy speaks to us. We know that we are not forgotten, that our cries have been heard.

Remembrance awakens us, dispersing the clouds that surround us. His remembrance is a promise that is fulfilled, a gift that is given. His remembrance is more powerful than any of our practices. Yet the collective focus on our individual self denies us full access to this light and love. His remembrance is always present but our collective attitude creates a barrier that surrounds us, a conditioning that cuts us off. We remain within the self-oriented world of our conditioned imagining, without a conscious relationship even to the idea of His remembrance; thus we negate the power of His remembrance.

We live in the world our conditioning has created, not even knowing that this "reality" is just a figment of our imaginings, an image of the world born from a self-oriented forgetfulness of the divine. "They forgot God so He forgot them" (Qur'an 9:67) is a powerful reminder of the dangers that engulf us, and yet the deeper tragedy is that we do not even know the degree of our forgetfulness. We do not know that we have created an image of life in which His remembrance of us is absent.

He who is always present, who is "closer to you than your very neck vein," has been banished to the heavens. And we remain alone, unaware of the poverty of our self-imposed isolation. The intimate relationship of the Creator and His creation has been lost, forgotten in the debris of our progress. When we remember Him we consciously connect with His ever-present power. When we forget Him we stand alone, far more susceptible to the negative influence of the collective, its prejudices, its ability to manipulate our integrity. Without the power of His presence to protect us, the demands of our lower nature and its many desires and fears attack us, influencing us to live in a way that is harmful to ourself and others.

The hearts of His lovers have never forgotten Him. His remembrance awoke them to their real nature, and His remembrance sustains them. Their hearts are alive only because of the intoxicating sweetness of His glance. They know that their whole existence depends upon His grace. Now His lovers are needed to reclaim the power of His remembrance for the collective and to use it as a sword to break up the negative forces that surround and influence us. Then His remembrance can dispel the darkness of our forgetfulness:

> We are like the night, earth's shadow.
> He is the Sun: He splits open the night with a sword
> soaked in dawn.[6]

Effort and Grace

How can there be an effort with divine things? They are given as a gift.

Bhai Sahib[1]

THE NEED FOR GRACE

Those who want to make the journey back to God need to know that only His grace can take us home. We need His love to melt us, His grace to transform us. We need to be opened and remade, our heart intoxicated with His tenderness, our soul nourished with His nearness. We need to be lifted out of ourself and brought into the presence of our Beloved.

Stepping onto the path, we step into the grace of a spiritual tradition, the power of love that is given for the work that needs to be done. This love is the foundation of any Sufi group, of any company of the friends of God. The grace is given effortlessly; it flows from heart to heart. Through this grace the miracle of transformation happens; the human being opens to discover something infinitely precious that is always present yet so easily hidden. Through His grace we come to realize how everything is according to His will, and we feel the completeness of His love for us.

Many sincere seekers do not know how lost they are without Him. Through effort we work upon ourself; we diligently practice our meditation, prayers, austerities, or other exercises. We strive towards the goal for which we long, aspiring to conquer our mind and body, transcend our limited self. The more we aspire the more we try to push ourself further, using our will-power to open the doors of revelation. Yet often we have no notion that these doors can only be opened from the other side, and that our need, our inadequacy, our despair, are what attract the help we need.

Sadly, many people struggle sincerely for years on the path without knowing that without His grace they cannot arrive even at the "first waystation." Through our own effort we may be able to purify ourself, to change certain habits and attitudes, to begin to practice meditation. But this is just the work of preparation and can only take us so far. We may appear to be growing and changing, but this is insignificant compared to the real journey, the real turning of the heart. But how does someone who knows only her own effort comprehend the necessity of grace? How can one whose life centers around herself detect the luminosity that glows just beyond the corner of her world?

Our heart knows what is missing, and it reveals its secrets in the most subtle ways. We might feel a cold shadow of despair that grows barely noticed in the night. Or sense something arid within us that our own love and tears cannot make fertile. Maybe we realize that our efforts are not quite effective, despite our deep longing to offer something of value, to give rise to something new. Maybe, in the busiest moments, out of the corner of our eye, we catch sight of a figure who beckons us to follow, who seems to know a secret just beyond our understanding. What would happen if we stopped to look more closely? What would happen if we allowed ourselves to be led away?

The Sufi is one who has tasted His power and His love and thus knows the limitation of her own efforts. Living in the presence of God, surrendered to His love, the lover's whole existence is founded upon the knowledge of His grace and the extent of her need for Him. When you have experienced the depth of your own poverty and tasted the abundance of His offering, you come to know that you can do nothing without His help. You cannot take one step along the path without His hand. You need Him to guide and support you, nourish and encourage you. Only your Beloved can give you what you need. Only He knows the ways of your heart and only His love can remove the veils of separation.

Within a circle of the friends of God this is the miracle that happens. As the light hidden within the heart begins to shine, a softness melts away the edges of our defenses. Everything is given as a gift; how can it be otherwise? How can we come close to our Beloved without His love to draw us to Him? While the seeker might use her own effort to free herself from old patterns and offer herself in service, the mystic knows that real transformation can happen only through His grace. Only through His grace can something open within the heart, can the path become visible. Without His grace we remain locked in the prison of the ego, in the illusions of our own self.

THE WORK ETHIC

Western culture teaches us to depend solely on ourselves, teaches us that our success or failure in all aspects of our lives is primarily self-determined. In North America this attitude is combined with a puritan work ethic which stresses the importance of effort and ignores the gift of grace. As with many aspects of collective conditioning this attitude is so pervasive that we don't question it. The focus on individual effort is so much a part of our landscape that we don't notice what is missing.

A work ethic has very productive material results, and can propel a person towards a dream of prosperity. Working hard, we can accomplish much on the physical plane—our efforts can be visibly rewarded. The American dream is a powerful incentive, and we are encouraged by hearing the "success stories" of others. But spiritual life functions quite differently. To know that His grace is the foundation for life creates an atmosphere completely different from that of the everyday world. When someone lives the fullness of what is given, the completeness of being inwardly supported, she puts the values of the world aside. A prayer by an American Confederate soldier seriously disabled in the Civil War illustrates how a material dream became transformed:

> I asked God for strength, that I might achieve;
> I was made weak, that I might learn humbly to obey.
> I asked for health, that I might do great things,
> I was given infirmity, that I might do better things.
> I asked for riches, that I might be happy;
> I was given poverty, that I might be wise.
> I asked for power, that I might have the praise of
>   men,
> I was given weakness that I might feel the need of
>   God.
> I asked for all things, that I might enjoy life;
> I was given life that I might enjoy all things.
> I got nothing I asked for—but everything I had
>   hoped for.
> Almost despite myself, my unspoken prayers were
>   answered.
> I am, among all men, most richly blessed.

This inversion of values speaks of a reality very distinct from our expectations, a reality in which we look at life from the perspective of what is given, rather than what we can accomplish. The dervish lives this relationship to life and God:

> A bedouin was asked, "Do you acknowledge the Lord?"
>
> He replied, "How could I not acknowledge Him who has sent me hunger, made me naked and impoverished, and caused me to wander from country to country?" As he spoke thus, he entered a state of ecstasy.

The Confederate soldier and the bedouin know that in the world of appearances abundance and destitution are just states of mind. When one understands that everything is given from God, experiences always point to a deeper opportunity, a deeper reality. Living beyond the superficiality of likes and dislikes, of good experiences and bad experiences, the dervish can keep her attention on God and the love that encircles them both. What is given to us shapes our path, and how we prepare for and receive what is given is our real contribution. The mystical path is an immersion in the "blessings" and "ecstasy" that come from within and are experienced only as aspects of a relationship in which everything comes from the Beloved.

Everything is given, everything can be taken away. All is a gift from our Beloved. But how can we recognize His gift when we are focused upon our own effort? How can we allow ourself to be lost and to be found? How can we learn to live in this way when we are conditioned to depend upon ourself?

SPIRITUAL PURIFICATION

Spiritual effort can achieve tangible results. Drawn by a longing for something other than the values of the world, we search for a path. We are awakened to the possibility of real freedom, of finding inner peace, of experiencing a love that is not caught in attachment. A path provides practices and spiritual teachings that help us change our attitude and still our mind. These practices if done diligently are powerful and productive, and can produce real results. We begin to discover that we can be a better person, have spiritual insights, have experiences in meditation.

Through our effort our aspirations begin to be answered. Something within us opens and responds to our searching. Through our practices, our study of spiritual teachings, and our participation in a spiritual community, we create a container. This container protects us from our lower nature and allows us to connect with the finer qualities that are often hidden within us. We begin to be nourished by these finer qualities, and discover compassion, generosity, tranquility, self-worth, or personal power. The density of worldly thought-forms and attitudes begins to be permeated with the light that comes from within.

As we continue to work upon ourself we are able to live more in tune with our real nature. Our outer and inner life benefit as we change and open, and often more energy is released. We may sense a joy, happiness, love, or spiritual well-being that is new and exciting. Our aspirations are rewarded, encouraging us to progress with our practices.

The novice can become ecstatic about the changes that are happening to her body, psyche, and mind, as a fundamental shift takes place. Just as a diet can release physical toxins, so can spiritual practices release mental and psychological toxins. Certain energy practices can be emotionally liberating, as inner barriers break down. Energy and feelings that had been repressed become accessible to consciousness.

The seeker also becomes aware of another reality quite different from that of the sensory world. She experiences the excitement of a new adventure, of discovering a self that is not burdened by all the psychological problems we carry. New horizons are revealed that point towards a more complete quality of life, an expanded consciousness. These are real and valuable experiences, signposts on the journey. However, what we do not realize is that these experiences are often just a preliminary "high," a spiritual honeymoon; most of them belong to the ego. At the beginning we are aware only of the ego; we are not open to higher levels of consciousness. These initial experiences are given to the ego to encourage us to pursue our path. They may appear liberating, but they are not the transformation of the heart, the expansion of the soul, that is the real essence of the mystical journey.

After the first few years these initial experiences often dry up. The work of purification continues but there is little tangible result. Seekers in this stage can become discouraged, even bitter. Where are the experiences that inspired them? What are the fruits of their efforts? Some become disillusioned with the path, while others may increase their efforts. They focus on their practices more diligently, and may even try to recreate their earlier enthusiasm, not realizing that the ego cannot nourish them any further. The glimpses given to the ego, the initial effects of spiritual purification, have worn away, and the seeker is left just with herself.

Wayfarers who began their journey with a taste of a higher truth can begin to lose their inner focus when they encounter this desert. The same is also true of some spiritual communities which start with an influx of energy which then dries up. After the initial idealism, shadow dynamics surface, and there is no longer the fire of continued spiritual experiences to counter what can be a destructive energy. Some communities fall apart while others remain bonded by their rituals, though an inertia begins to develop under the surface. The spiritual focus dissipates; the joy of the path becomes lost.

This disillusionment is valid. One cannot continue sustained either by early enthusiasm or by effort. Rituals and practices can take one only so far. A spiritual community is only a container. If something within the heart is not being nourished, nothing new can be born. The seeker must make the transition from being focused on effort to being receptive to grace or she will remain in the sphere of the ego where there is no rebirth and no journey.

THE KEEPER OF THE GATES OF GRACE

On the Sufi path everything is given through the grace of the *sheikh*, the Sufi term for spiritual master or guide. The *sheikh* is the keeper of the gates of grace, and the wayfarer needs this grace to make the journey Home, to become dissolved in love, lost in the infinite ocean of the Beloved. This is why the Sufi says that you need a guide, a master of the path of love. Only through the grace that comes through the *sheikh* can you be turned inside out, transformed, melted, merged into the divine oneness.

What is this power, this energy, this divine love that does not belong to the world? Why do we need it?

What calls us to it and how do we recognize it? To all of these questions there is the one answer: "The heart knows." Sufis work through the heart; they understand the secret mysteries of the heart and how the power of divine love can activate this inner organ of higher consciousness. Through the heart we are given the energy we need for the journey:

> The disciple progresses through love. Love is the driving force, the greatest power of creation. As the disciple has not enough love in him to have sufficient of the propelling power to reach the goal, so love is increased, or "created" simply by activating the heart chakra.[2]

The activation of the heart *chakra* can only be done by a master of the path (or by his representative), by someone who understands the ways of love, and who has been given permission to do this work. In the words of a Sufi master, "We are simple people. But we can turn the heart of a human being so that human being will go on and on, where nobody can even imagine it."[3]

The *sheikh* is a transformer of divine power. If we were to directly access the Absolute we would be destroyed by Its tremendous, unlimited power. Just as a transformer is needed to make electricity in the high voltage mains usable in our house without blowing every fuse, so does the *sheikh* give us access to the divine energy in amounts we can assimilate.

This energy is given from heart to heart, from soul to soul. The *sheikh* has access to the place within our heart that belongs to God, the heart of hearts. Our *sheikh* has the key to this secret chamber, and as the agent of the Beloved infuses it with the secret substance of divine consciousness, *sirr*, then nourishes this substance with grace. Our work of purification cleans out the debris of our lower nature and prepares the chamber of the heart, so that the work of His love can take place without being corrupted.

Each in our own way we are taken to God. Through our devotion, aspiration, and ceaseless attention we attract the grace of the *sheikh*, without which there can be no miracle of transformation. His grace holds us in our aloneness, contains us in our tears. The *sheikh* is one who has been made empty, and through him we are taken into the arena of our own non-being, to taste the deeper truth of our divine nature. Through the grace of our *sheikh* we learn how to become nothing, to give ourself totally to our Beloved:

> The lover must be like a dead body in the hands of the Beloved. How is the dead body? Helpless it is. If it is put in the rain, it gets wet; if it is put in the sun, it gets hot. It cannot rebel, it cannot protest. And it is by the grace of the guru that we are learning how to be always contented in the hands of the Beloved.[4]

THE NEED OF THE SOUL

He is one, and His relationship to His creation is oneness. His oneness is a fundamental reality that the mystic knows within the heart. Everything is contained within His presence, nourished by His love. Without His sustaining presence creation would cease to exist. We are a part of Him, and He gives us what we need. Our need attracts His grace. This is why the Sufi says, "There must be need. There must be need."

When we are needy we cry to Him, and He answers. The cry of the lover hungry for love goes from heart to heart. "Light rises towards light and light comes down upon light. And it is *Light upon Light*."[5] But if we are unaware of our need then we deny our access to His grace. Instead, we remain isolated within the sphere of our own efforts.

Consciousness is very powerful and has the potential to attract or to obstruct. If we consciously look towards Him, our heart opens and our need is carried to Him on our prayer. If we do not know what we need, if our consciousness remains focused upon ourself or our material world, then we create a barrier between ourself and His help. Consciousness can be a prison as much as it can create a connection. When we are focused upon ourself we turn away from Him whose grace we need. When we value only our own effort we reject His help.

For the Sufi the attitude of the wayfarer is very important. Although Sufism is a path of surrender this is not a passive surrender. The lover who gives herself unconditionally to love is an active partner. Her attitude of devotion, the way she looks towards her Beloved—whether He appears present or absent—attracts His attention. Mysticism is a relationship of love in which the lover, through her need and helplessness, calls upon her Beloved, attracts His attention, and brings His love into the world. Without the active participation of the lover, without her giving herself to her need for His love, there would be no relationship, no call and no answer. The lover is the magnet that attracts His love. "Heaven says to the earth, 'Hallo! Thou drawest me like iron to a magnet!'"[6]

Collectively we are caught in patterns of denial and isolation. Collectively we reject the need of the soul. The work ethic that we have inherited has its dark side; it does not allow us to be vulnerable and weak, to need our invisible Beloved. The feminine side of love, receptivity and longing, is neither valued nor understood. We are taught to struggle, not to surrender. And since we do not recognize our need we do not know that His grace is present.

How can we ask for His grace when we are conditioned to believe that only our own efforts can help us? As a culture we have forgotten that we can only be taken to God by God, and that our need for Him is His need for us:

> Remember what the soul wants,
> because in that, eternity
> is *wanting* our souls!
>
> Which is the meaning of the text,
> *They love That, and That loves them.*[7]

In the oneness of love our longing for Him is His longing for us; lover and Beloved share the heart's desire for union. But we will never give ourselves to this oneness, to His need and longing, when we know only ourself. We will never know the place where His grace is when we only look to ourself.

His lovers carry the seed of remembrance and are awakened to the depth of their own need. They have felt their heart cry to Him, and know that this call is answered, even though they often have to wait, to be patient. They know that they cannot walk a single step along the path without His grace. And they know how He longs to help those who look towards Him, to love those who long for Him. The need of the soul is His gift, just as the sorrow of the heart is His mark. He knows that we cry for His sake:

Of all those tears and cries and supplications
I was the magnet, and I gave them wings.[8]

THE BETRAYAL OF A DREAM

We can no longer afford to muffle the cry of the soul, to
deny our need for grace. The gates of grace are there for
those who call to Him, for those who allow His wings to
lift their tears. The masters of love and their helpers are
always present in the world, responding to the need of
the time and the place and the people. Much of their
work is done on the inner planes, where there are no
limitations of time and space. They guide the currents of
love, the flow of grace, to where heart cries, soul needs.
When we look towards Him our consciousness becomes
a light that attracts the attention of those who are here
to help us. Our supplication pierces the dense thought-
forms of the collective that cover us. But without this
focus of intention, the help that can be given is less
accessible. The power of consciousness is not present;
light does not rise towards light.

But if we do not know the existence of His grace,
how can we ask? If we have been conditioned to believe
only in the value of our own effort, how can we recognize
the need of the soul? Without His grace the transformation of the heart cannot take place; there can be no real
spiritual journey. All the well-intentioned effort, the
initial experiences, do not take us anywhere. The seeker
remains with the sadness of an unfulfilled dream, an
unlived potential. There can be bitterness, even anger,
at what never happened.

The greatest promise given to a human being is the
possibility to go Home, to make the journey of the soul.
This is the birthright of every wayfarer. If this journey is

obscured by the ignorance of the collective, a deep betrayal takes place within the soul. And yet His grace is
always present. In the circle of His oneness nothing can
be hidden from Him. Even if we do not ask, we are given
to. Even if we are deaf to our soul's need, He hears its cry.
We always have the opportunity to turn towards Him.
But if we do not know the nature of our need, we can not
be fully receptive to the grace that is present.

Individually and collectively we are the co-creators
of our own destiny; we have the free will to choose our
fate. We can ask for the help we need, or remain within
our own ego-centered world. We carry His longing within
our heart, just as we carry the secret of His oneness. We
can chose to live this consciously, awakened by remembrance, looking towards Him. Then the soul sings and
we live its song, seeing the path in front of us, surrender-
ing more and more to the wonder of His grace. Or we can
remain forgetful of who we are, even as His love is present.

Completeness

Knowing is passing from the false to the true
And seeing the Absolute Whole in the part.

Shabistarî

THE COMPLETENESS OF LIFE

This world has a quality of completeness that is threatening to rational consciousness. The mystic knows that He is one and that His world reflects His oneness. In His oneness everything is complete and whole. This completeness is a quality of every atom of creation, of everything that is stamped with His name. The mystic experiences this completeness as a deep feeling of well-being, that everything is as it should be.

And yet the mystic lives in a world governed by rationality, a masculine mode of thinking that is analytic and linear rather than holistic. Perceiving only the parts within the whole, incapable of knowing the oneness of life, the rational mind is confronted by the inequities and discord of the world. It works to organize and make sense of what it perceives, solve the problems it confronts.

How does the mystic reconcile the two, the mystical knowledge that everything is according to His will and reflects His oneness, and the visible signs of disharmony—the incompleteness that appears within us and in the life that surrounds us? While it might be tempting to simply turn away from the world, or impose some image of divine order upon it, the mystic does neither. She lives amidst the chaos and beauty of life and sees it as it is. She is a realist who has passed behind the veil of appearances and knows that the hidden oneness of life reveals itself in a paradoxical way.

The mystic is someone who has surrendered to the unknowable essence of existence. She has stepped outside of the parameters of the rational mind, and does not seek to impose any image upon life. The mystic lives unrestricted by conditioning and experiences life directly without an imposed pattern of consciousness, without judgment or a framework of beliefs. Mystical consciousness is a state of being, and in this state of being the real nature of life is experienced: the oneness and completeness of His creation are lived, even in the midst of the seeming conflict and fragmentation of His world.

Rational consciousness does not allow this paradox. It protects us from what we cannot understand, and in so doing keeps us from the reality beyond the ego. While it helps us to define our place in the world, and navigate our way through its practical dimension, its fundamental limitation is that it perceives the world from the perspective of the mind and the ego. From this perspective it interprets the world according to its values and parameters, its need for order and progress. It creates a limited image of life that it can attempt to understand and categorize, and cuts us off from experiencing the unknowable vastness of life. Its patterns of thought do not allow us to live in the moment or appreciate the compeletness of life that is always present. Instead we are driven by the goals we have created, not even knowing that these goals are just images in our mind.

PRECONCEPTIONS ABOUT THE PATH

One can best understand the power of these patterns in one's own life. For the seeker it may be played out in relationship to the path. Many of us push ourself forward along an image of the path, a path of exertion that leads towards a goal. We search for order, try to understand what is happening in our life, what forces are at play. We try to give a sense of coherence to what disturbs us, to validate our suffering with a sense of purpose. But gradually it dawns that this is just an excuse, a pretense to keep us from what is real, from a life that cannot be understood but can be lived. We come to discover that like life, the path is a strange creature, full of the unexpected, attempting to take us into the unknown, the unknowable, the completeness of His presence.

Patterns of avoidance take many forms, have many disguises. And yet what we seek to avoid is always with us, and is often the key that unlocks the wholeness we have forgotten, the vastness from which we would hide ourself. As human beings we contain so many contradictions. We are caught between heaven and earth, and can sense the wonder and futility of our own existence. Mystical reality does not seek to contain these contradictions—in the infinite ocean of His love they are all present. Instead, the mystic is happy to lose all context for understanding, to forget any imposed restrictions of knowing.

When we approach this infinite ocean certain changes take place, changes that are both organic and devastating. How we continue to lead our life depends upon how we assimilate these changes, how much we allow ourself to lose and how much we allow ourself to be given. And our mind is a part of this process. We cannot just dismiss our mind because of its limitations. On the Sufi path the "mind is hammered into the heart," meaning that it comes to function in a different way— in harmony with our soul. We have to adjust to a consciousness that is not rational and yet has a simplicity and depth of understanding that includes rationality.

The mystic is driven by a need to understand her own limitations and tries to push her mind beyond them, to assimilate a different picture. We search to discover what the heart has always known, that there are no boundaries to love, and we are left, frightened, on the edge of our expectations, unaware of the simplicity of the unknown. For so long we have searched, hoping, expecting, to find something. Is it a realization that we have longed for? Is it a meeting with a lost lover? We stand on the precipice, looking out over the horizon of ourself. Yet, in our own inner emptiness, our day-by-day existence, there is no answer, but the death of a question. Here there is no seeking, no lover lost and found. There is no looking, nothing to reach for, no path to follow.

Always we thought that there was something to seek, a journey to make. Now we know it is otherwise. There is the passion of day-to-day life. But the source brings something else to the surface, something we need to nourish rather than define. There is a bigger wholeness hidden, waiting at the corner of the moments, watching from behind the thoughts. This wholeness has an unexpected purpose. From across time and beyond space, it has a scent, indistinguishable and yet distinct, like a wine that has been fermented *elsewhere* and retains that quality.

We have been waiting for something to happen, and yet the happening has come closer. We sense another presence, another pattern, unhidden but unrevealed. There is a tender sense of silence, without prayer to or from. In the moments of our own silence we are welcomed, as both stranger and friend. We need to allow this presence to be with us, not in defined moments, but as a flow. The river is here, not hidden behind the bank or crossing the horizon. The silence, unbidden, is always present. It carries the quality of walled gardens where the roses bloom in abundance. In the tranquility of the moment there is no moment, nothing defined or captured. This world is seeped with the other, soaked with the dew of timelessness.

We thought that prayer was a relationship of us and God, us and the teacher, us and another. But we were wrong. Prayer just is. In that *isness* everything is included. Us, the Beloved, the object of our prayer, and the will to unfold the eternal into the present, to cross the borders of time and space, drench the now with eternity. There is no other. We are always alone but we thought it was a state of incompleteness. We waited for someone to come. How can there be another when He is *one?*

The world spins around a place of silence and waiting. We need to enter this silence, and wait in the eternal present in which there is no future. The days unfold in their own majesty of sunrise and sunset, yet we so easily miss that magic moment when non-being comes into existence, sheds its skin of invisibility and begins the dance that some call life. The waves of non-existence crash against the shores of being, but we need to watch with the corner of our eyes. Only then can we see what is whirling out of the timeless. And yet for Him we are always unprepared. Our knowledge is our own undoing. Our preoccupations prepare us for what we already know, and thus are useless. Life is too vast to be contained by anything except a heart steeped in love.

ONENESS AND DISCRIMINATION

The path takes us to a place of completeness, to the mystery of everything being given. But how do we live this, how do we bring it into our daily life without distortion? How can we avoid our rational self with its images of order that try to protect us from chaos? In fullness everything is included, accepted, part of the whole. There is no division or contradiction, just a continual interaction. Life is, and we are a part of its unfolding. And our rational self too is included, but only as one facet, one aspect of our experience. The danger comes when we limit our possibilities, when we select the life we want rather than giving ourself to the life that is.

Chaos and order, love and sorrow—we are surrounded by seeds of so many possibilities. The mind wants to select only a few, to present us with a linear picture of our life and its potential. But the lover who looks with the eyes of passion does not want to limit love, does not want to deny tears. For lovers there is neither chaos nor order; passion does not exist in straight lines, but takes us over the edge of ourself. Those who are addicted to order cannot make sense of love, nor can they give themselves to life. Lovers are friends with the abyss, with the moments in which everything can be lost or a single glance can recapture paradise.

Giving ourself to love, we surrender to a completeness that holds and takes us. It takes us beyond ourself, beyond any pattern we might think to impose. Love is quicker than the mind so it leaves thinking behind, though thinking may try to catch up, to understand what is happening. But love just *is*, and the mystic is someone who is immersed in love's *isness*. We are held captive by love, and the mind is marooned elsewhere, struggling with what it cannot understand. Lovers know this with a knowledge that comes from being drunk, from that momentary ecstasy of annihilation when what is free and unlimited slips into consciousness.

Love is chaos and beauty, passion and poverty. When we are taken by love out of ourself, love saturates us with the perfume of our own non-existence. Love can never be limited, just as the heart's sorrow is endless. The mystic lives with a consciousness attuned to love, waiting for love, watching for her Beloved. The mind of the mystic is immersed in love, just as any lover is absorbed with thoughts of her beloved. Love alters the mind, changes its patterns. In the mind of the lover two become one, ecstasy happens. And this is real, not just empty fantasy. Love brings the mind into the heart and trains it in the ways of oneness.

Yet we live in a world of limitation, full of misunderstanding and confusion. The oneness of the heart is often veiled in the outer world, and the lover has to confront the difficulties that arise in everyday life. Within the heart the opposites are united; sorrow and joy come together. But in the outer world we have to discriminate, to live what is true to ourself and turn away from compromises that could condition us. We have to separate right from wrong, and at the same time hold the oneness in which everything is included. Without judgment or recrimination we have to walk the path of our own nature, knowing its limitations and yet living its essential purity.

For the lover the only absolute is the Beloved. In this world He whom we love has so many faces, so many ways of manifestation. We try to see how He reveals Himself, what aspect of Him comes to meet us in our daily life. We try not to reject any face of our Beloved, however He may appear. We know the limitations of our own judgment, and yet at the same time have to use the tools of discrimination, exercise our freedom to choose. The mind needs to be trained to discriminate according to our inner nature, so that the light of our Higher Self can be used to guide us.

He who is not limited, who is freedom itself, often comes to us in ways we could easily reject. So many times He gives us the opportunity to become free of the patterns of our conditioning, drawing us into unexpected and unwelcome situations. If we use the light of our love, we can see behind the veil of our expectations and judgments. In this way He can reveal Himself to us more completely, and we can share in the mystery of His creation.

To stay true to love and to the needs of our Beloved is a work of continual attention. So often we slip back into familiar patterns and so miss an opportunity. These patterns protect us from our own vulnerability and insecurity, from the aloneness of being with God. Our patterns shield us from the bright light of burning truth and from taking real responsibility for ourself and the need of the moment. Conditioned responses are so subtle and pervasive: we respond automatically most of the time. But the lover has tasted the freedom within the heart and needs to live this calling, to be open to the unlimited whilst living in a world of limitation.

Gradually freedom and the discrimination of the heart become part of our life. We follow the ways of love, never knowing the next step. Sometimes there are hints that prepare us, but so often we are blind, trusting only Him whom we cannot see.

Our Beloved is always with us, but we know that He is often hidden. He does not always reveal Himself in the world, just as He veils Himself within our own heart. When He is hidden we have to stand alone and make our own judgments and sometimes we make mistakes. But

His mercy is greater than His justice, and even when we fail Him He does not forget us. The unconditional nature of His love is hard to understand in a world of rationality.

RATIONALITY AND DIRECT PERCEPTION

He hides and reveals Himself. When He reveals Himself we can feel the completeness of life, that everything is just as He wills. When He hides Himself we are left with the fragmented sense of our own self, with our feelings of incompleteness and our need to find what is missing, what is absent. But as our mind is trained by love we are able to glimpse Him more often. Our rational conditioning stops cutting us off and we trust more and more our deeper knowing, our sense of His presence.

We want to live in the space where everything is present and we feel the wholeness of our being. Yet time and time again we are thrown back to the fragmented nature of the ego, with its unmet needs and distorted perceptions of life. Within the sphere of the ego we know our incompleteness and try to find what is missing. We are haunted by our unlived dreams, and search for them in the inner and outer world. This is what draws us deep into ourself and also throws us into life. Sometimes we think what is missing can be found in a partner, or in a successful career. Or looking inward we may hope to release blocked creativity that gives us access to a fuller expression of ourself, a richer participation in life. Always we look for what is missing, and this is how the soul draws us into the experiences we need, the life that it wants us to taste.

But the very nature of the ego is that it will always remain fragmented; it can never embrace the whole.

When we come to know the ego's dark twin, our rejected or repressed shadow self, we experience a greater whole-ness, and from this comes a more profound sense of well-being, a fuller interaction with life. But this is only a limited perception of ourself, and the mystic always knows that only He can make us whole. The ego will always live within its defined world, while the lover car-ries the memory of a lost love that does not belong to time or space.

Each time He deserts us we search for Him; each time He abandons us we cry for Him. The danger comes when His absence throws us back into the familiar patterns of rational consciousness, when we leave the vulnerability of our tears and feelings of abandonment for the security of the known. Rational consciousness provides an escape from the terrible insecurity of belonging to God. We so easily slip back into these familiar thought-forms that offer a defined view of life and of what is real. The mind cuts us off from the uncharted waters of love, from its ter-rible storms and blood-red sunsets.

Then we begin to doubt the nature of our inner connection, of the heart's belonging. We may even doubt that we are on the path, that we are allowed to know His love. When the rational mind gets hold of our longing it can twist it into depression; it can turn our tears into self-pity. Reason can make us doubt our own devotion, and finally deny us access to our own heart.

The mind loves arguments, and the more we fight it the more energy we give to this battle. We remain within the sphere of the mind with arguments and counter-arguments. So much energy is drawn into this inner ex-change that we have little left for the path. Our inner dialogue absorbs us and we can no longer keep our atten-tion on the heart. Then even when the Beloved returns, when He unveils Himself, we do not notice. We are busy battling old demons, engaged in useless inner conflicts. The totality of His love passes us by—it does not fit into any framework of argument.

How can we escape this self-destructive cycle that seems to afflict so many seekers? How can we avoid wasting so much energy? The mind is "the slayer of the Real," and a well-educated mind has many tools at its disposal. It can easily convince us of the hopelessness of our love affair, persuade us that we will never make the journey. It knows our limitations and feelings of inadequacy and parades them in front of us. But there is a basic flaw in the arguments of the mind: the mind cannot see that everything is according to His will.

The mystic is born with a quality of direct perception that *knows* that everything is according to His will. This direct perception may become covered by the conditioning of rational consciousness, but it remains under the surface, in a dormant state, until His grace and the container of the path awaken it.

Direct perception functions through the heart rather than the mind. It is the quality of consciousness with which we can see His face wheresoever we turn. Direct perception functions at a higher frequency than the rational mind, which is why the rational mind cannot grasp it. Nor can the collective condition our direct perception. If we remain on the level of the rational mind we are caught in its sphere of arguments and doubts. But once the mystical perception is awakened we have access to this higher frequency, which cannot be contaminated—it moves too fast for slower rational thought-forms to grasp hold of it.

Once the heart is awakened it looks towards God, and with the eye of the heart we can see His oneness within life, His face in the world. The heart knows that everything happens according to His will, that it cannot be otherwise.

The work of the mystic is to stay true to this inner knowing of the heart and surrender the mind to its understanding. Then we escape from the futile arguments of reason that can sap so much of our energy. We become more and more attuned to the faster consciousness of the heart and have access to its direct understanding. The consciousness of the heart is in harmony with all of life because it belongs to God. It knows the wholeness of creation, the completeness that is present in each and every moment.

PROGRESS AND REVELATION

The mystic does not deny the idea of progress or evolution. The wayfarer experiences changes within herself as she journeys along the path. Consciousness expands and she has access to more energy and a more profound understanding of herself and life. Nor does she disparage external progress: being part of humanity, she welcomes any lessening of suffering, more access to freedom, education, food. She recognizes the profound changes happening in the world, how we are being given more opportunities than ever before. She works to help us to understand and grow with these changes, to use the gifts we are being given for our greater benefit rather than greed or self-degradation.

As much as the mystic is immersed in the present, she is also working for the future. The Sufi master Bhai Sahib expresses this seeming paradox:

Why not realize here and now in this life. Why think of later? Only the moment of NOW matters...

True, we all work for the future, ultimately, what else? Otherwise you wouldn't be here but think of NOW ONLY; forget tomorrow.[1]

In the present moment the lover aspires to give herself more completely to God, and is in service to help humanity realize its divine potential. Part of the work of the mystic is to help humanity adjust and grow with the changes that are about to take place. The mystic knows that these changes first happen on the inner planes, before they come into manifestation. Through our meditation and inner work we are able to tune into this potential for change before it manifests. We have learned how to let dreams and intuitions guide us so that we move with the changes of this life, rather than resist or impede our own self-development. Through warning dreams or hints we learn how to avoid negative situations.

Our work as mystics is to keep our inner alignment, whatever the changes in our outer life, and we do this for ourself and the world. The wisdom of Kipling's "If"—

If you can keep your head when all about you
Are losing theirs and blaming it on you

—is a basic practice for the mystic. Because we are attuned to the dynamic currents that flow into life, we are a part of these changes before they happen on the outer planes. And because we have learned to become inwardly free from the limitations of form or identity, we do not get caught in patterns that could obstruct change.

The inner attention of the mystic, her awareness of the signs of change, enables her to keep the connection between the worlds. She is not thrown into discord by the changes that take place, nor is she caught in any collective hysteria or fear. She learns to remain a still

point in the turning world, a center of stability and alignment. The value of such people in our turbulent times
cannot be overestimated.

Through her inner attention she is also able to grasp
the real potential of any change: what it has to offer
humanity. The path has taught her not to be attached to
appearances, but to see a situation within her own life
from an inner perspective, grasp what is being reflected
by the outer event. The mystic knows that real evolution
is the evolution of consciousness, as that is what determines our experience of life. She knows this from her
own journey, and thus is able to see its potential within
the collective. As our consciousness evolves, so we are
able to grasp more of the wholeness of life: see more
colors of the spectrum.

External progress without the evolution of consciousness has little value. We can so easily destroy the
civilization that we have built. A few days of bombing
can throw back a country by half a century or more. In
the thirteenth century the Sufis worked to rebuild the
Middle East after the hordes of Ghengis Khan put back
civilization by two hundred years. But changes of consciousness remain, whatever the external circumstance.
Changes of consciousness radically affect the real quality of our life, as the mystic knows from her own experience.

The work of the mystic is to hold the potential for
a change in consciousness. Evolution of consciousness
allows a more complete revelation: we can see Him more
clearly and more fully within His creation. The mystic
knows that the real purpose of progress is revelation. We
experience this on our own journey; as we progress along
the path, we glimpse more of the wonder of our Beloved,
we come closer to experiencing the essential oneness of
life and love.

Our culture has become so identified with linear progress, with its defined goals, that it has forgotten the miracle of revelation. Western civilization sees progress as a goal itself, and is so caught up in activity that it is not receptive to the possibilities of real change. For example, the present revolution in communication is regarded more as a means for a global market than for global consciousness. Thus the future remains within the framework of the past, easily polluted by greed and ego-desires, and we have lost the opportunity for a leap in our collective consciousness.

The mystic who lives amidst the activities of the marketplace and yet is inwardly attentive knows that a certain new energy is being made available. The signs are all around us. This energy is what is "speeding up" our present civilization and allowing for rapid developments in technology and ideas. But this is just a side effect. The real potential is a shift in consciousness.

In each age the completeness of life can reveal itself in a new way; a different divine attribute can become known, a different quality of His nature become part of our life. And yet humanity is given free will to accept or reject this change. What matters is that humanity be made conscious of the opportunity that is present. A new quality of thought needs to be constellated to help people to grasp this opportunity. If enough people are attentive to the inner dynamic of change, then we may be able to incarnate a new quality of consciousness. The alternative is to use the energy made available to foster further material or ego goals.

Within the heart of the world this new quality of thought is being formed, a thought that does not restrict or condition but embraces all of life. The mystic who works for love has access to this thought, and can bring it into being within herself. This thought is necessary for consciousness to develop, for this world to return to being a place of revelation. What will be revealed we cannot even imagine, because it belongs to a future born from the beyond. But there is a joy that is beginning to surface, a joy that speaks of what might happen. It is the joy of life returning to its simple essence of becoming, the spark in the heart awakening with love.

From heart to heart this seed of consciousness is being passed. It is alive and in need of attention. It is a child crying in the wilderness, a dream that stands at the edge of dawn. Many generations depend upon this moment, and yet all is according to His will. For lovers there is neither yesterday nor tomorrow, but a moment being made in time. If we touch this moment with awareness and receptivity, something can be given, can be made known. The heart knows the completeness of what is real, how everything is included. Love carries this knowledge and gives it to life.

Recognizing the Signs of God

All the world loves you, but you are nowhere to be found. Hidden and yet completely obvious.

Rûmî[1]

THE CONSTANTLY CHANGING CREATION

The mystic experiences this world as a place of divine revelation in which the Beloved comes to know Himself. This is a dynamic unfolding of love, a constantly evolving process of Self-disclosure. All of creation is a part of His Self-revelation, but only humanity has the capacity to consciously contribute to this process. And only someone who has given herself to God, whose heart has been awakened, is able to consciously recognize His signs as they are made known in the world and in herself. This is one of the deepest purposes of the mystic: to be able to recognize the constantly changing face of God. She carries this knowledge for humanity, holding the secrets of His love within the consciousness of her heart.

Through His signs He reveals His secret nature, the mystical truth of life. As life evolves, so this secret expresses itself in different ways, revealing different facets of the One Truth. He who is One and Alone reveals Himself in the multiplicity of His creation, a creation which is constantly evolving. His revelation of Himself is not a static event in time. Just as creation is a dynamic, continual process, so is His revelation, for "God never discloses Himself in a single form twice, nor in a single form to two individuals."[2] Each moment He reveals Himself in a new way; each moment His world manifests His revelation within the infinity of what is possible.

In our own journey of self-discovery we come to know ourself through the diversity of our interaction with life, through our many different acts, thoughts, feelings, emotions. The many different aspects of our inner and outer life gradually reveal to us our essential self, the single face reflected back in life's many-faceted mirror. For our own self, life is a journey of self-revelation, and we learn to read the signs that are within ourself and in our outer life. Catching the thread of our deeper destiny, we come to know the hidden purpose of our life. From the dance of opposites, inner and outer, feminine and masculine, the secrets of the soul become known.

We are made in the image of God and we reflect His process of Self-revelation. "He who knows himself knows his Lord." If we look upon our life with eyes awakened to truth, we discover not only our own nature, but also that of our Lord. For the Sufi, life is the greatest teacher. Through our life, through its constantly changing diversity, we come to know our own self and the divine within us. Oneness reveals itself though multiplicity. The mystic experiences this in her own life; she knows the wonder of Self-revelation.

Through her journey of self-discovery she becomes attuned to the hidden oneness, becomes fixed upon the essence of her being. The image of a wheel with many spokes looking towards the center, or an orchestra always attentive to the conductor, points to a dynamic relationship of the one to the many. The single center supports the multiplicity; but without the spokes of the wheel there would be no motion, without the members of the orchestra there would be no music. The center becomes manifest, reveals itself through the many.

Oneness and multiplicity reflect each other. Multiplicity points us back to oneness and oneness opens itself to us through life. And yet each revelation is unique, as a different quality of His oneness becomes known. "No one knows God but God," but He reveals to us His qualities, His names and attributes. What is hidden within the heart, the names of God, becomes manifest in our life. The mystic is one who has eyes to see this Self-revelation, to catch the thread of His unveiling. When the eye of the heart is opened and our consciousness is attuned to love, we see within the dance of creation. In the words of Ibn 'Arabî:

> How can I know You when You are the inwardly
>   Hidden who is not known?
> How can I not know You when You are the
>   outwardly Manifest who make
>   Yourself known to me in everything?[3]

A NEW WAY OF REVELATION

We are a part of creation and we carry the name of God in our heart. We are His secret and He is our secret. But in order for this secret to be made known within ourself we need to continually evolve, and in particular our consciousness needs to change. Otherwise we will not be able to recognize His signs, and His secret will remain unknown. Then the world will be starved of the sacred essence of Self-revelation. The divine will remain hidden, His secret unrevealed.

Although in each moment He reveals Himself in a new way, each age also has a particular quality of divine revelation. In each age there is a fundamental shift in the way the Oneness reveals itself. There was a time when the divine was revealed primarily through the ways of the goddess, and the priestesses held the secrets of divine perception. The many aspects of oneness were made known through the pantheon of gods and goddesses, and the initiates of the temples guided humanity by their dreams and visions. Then a new quality of divine consciousness arose, and a monotheistic culture appeared, often using the sword to announce its arrival. The priests of this culture recognized a transcendent divinity, and our relationship to the one God was established. The signs and symbols of this new revelation were distinct from the past, and the oracles of old could not read them. New religions were established to hold the divine consciousness of humanity, religions that embodied their wisdom in sacred texts. Revelation was carried by the word, *logos*, not just the secrets passed down to initiates.

For over two thousand years masculine consciousness has determined our collective relationship to the divine. It gave us a new way to come to know our transcendent nature, establishing a spiritual relationship to a reality that is beyond the physical world. Humanity's eyes and hearts were opened to a different quality of divine perception in which His oneness was celebrated. At the same time the masculine established its hierarchies and power structures, and a certain light gradually became distorted. His revelation lost its brightness. A magic essential to life became lost.

As we stand at the end of an era the old ways of relating to the divine no longer hold their promise. To create new forms is never the answer, nor can the past answer our need. Even though the secrets of the priestesses have a deep meaning, the ways of the goddess belong to a previous era. Our divine consciousness continually evolves, and we need to allow for something new to be born.

In each age there is a fundamental shift in the way the divine reveals itself. This shift has already taken place. His signs no longer reveal themselves in the old way. T.S. Eliot prefigured this in *The Wasteland* when he wrote:

What are the roots that clutch, what branches grow
Out of this stony rubbish? Son of man,
You cannot say, or guess, for you know only
A heap of broken images, where the sun beats,
And the dead tree gives no shelter, the cricket no
   relief,
And the dry stone no sound of water.[4]

If we look in the old ways we will not be able to recognize the signs of God, nor will we be able to read them and be nourished by them. We will be left with a "dead tree" and "stony rubbish." What is being born within the soul of the world is a quality of consciousness that comes from a union of masculine and feminine. We need to reclaim the feminine so that it can unite with the masculine in a new way, through which a new consciousness can be born, a new way of relating to life, enabling us to have a fuller understanding of our true nature and purpose. Then the deeper meaning of the feminine can become visible, the hidden purpose of the masculine enacted.

This new integration of masculine and feminine will affirm the direct perception of the heart, the mystical ability to see the Truth as it is revealed. What does this mean? The difficulty is that we cannot describe something new in the terminology of the past. We cannot define what has not yet been lived. We can only recog-

nize our need. If we do not awaken our new-born ability
to recognize the signs of God, we will miss this moment
of transition and remain in the desert of our impoverish-
ment which will only grow more desperate and arid. If
we recognize His signs, then a deep joy will return to life
as its spiritual essence is affirmed. What this means we
cannot even imagine.

The mystic, living in the moment, is always open to
that which is as yet unrealized, to what is in the process
of becoming. Free of conditioning, we are receptive to
what is new, both within ourself and within life. And the
mystic always carries an affirmation of what life gives, of
how our Beloved manifests Himself. We are awake to
what is hidden and what needs to be revealed. His lovers
have always kept open the gates of spiritual transformation, through which He is able to remember Himself
within the hearts of those who love Him.

The work of the mystic is to discover this new quality of divine consciousness within, and then establish it
both in her inner and in her outer life. This new consciousness needs to be lived if it is to take root and flourish.
Mystics have always stood at the forefront of consciousness, at the borders with the beyond where what is new
comes into being. Because they are not attached to form,
they can embrace what is as yet undefined, what carries
the fragrance of the future.

And yet many mystics are reluctant to take their
place in the world, to live the seeds of this change. Mystics
are often by nature reclusive, introvert, looking inward
towards the source. They are distrustful of collective
activity, knowing how easily the collective perverts and
distorts, how easily the subtle truths of the heart become
contaminated, lost. Often they have paid the price of
persecution, or carry this experience in their ancient
memories. They would rather live their truth inwardly

in the solitude of their own devotion, where the power structures of the collective cannot reach, where their knowledge is not condemned as heretical.

To establish a mystical consciousness within the collective is a dream that belongs to idiots and fools of God. The power structures of the present appear so solid, so successful. Lovers walk down the by-ways of life, where their love can be shared without the danger of discovery. They would rather cry in the wilderness of their own longing than in the desolation of the market-place. But there is a need for something to be made known, for the secrets of the heart to be made public, for the music of the soul to be played.

His lovers know that the path is not about self-improvement, that there is no ten-step program to God. They know the intensity and passion of their own heart, the windswept vistas of the soul. They have lived the price of longing and despair, have smelled the fragrance of His presence. And they know how easily this wonder can be corrupted, how subtle are the ways the ego fabricates an image of the path. And yet their natural inclination is to remain silent, to withdraw within their own devotion. No one can be converted to love. It is too free to be packaged, too potent to be forced.

But the need of the time is pressing. For centuries His lovers have held the secrets of divine love within their own hearts, shared only with initiates. But this knowledge needs to be made public, the song of His oneness to be heard. If the music of divine love is not played in the marketplace, life will lose its meaning, and the collective despair of the soul will be too terrible to imagine. Already there are signs of this happening, of an anguish that cannot be placated. And everywhere there spreads the cold fog of forgetfulness, the haunting desolation of a world that has forgotten its pledge to remember Him.

Without the signs of God we cannot find our way back. But who is here to discover the signs and then to read them for us? The priests of the established religions are no longer initiates, and their concern is often social welfare rather than awakening to the sacred. The oracles are long closed, the ancient temples just a memory. The signs are all around us but we do not know how to read them. Our attention is so caught in the grip of the outer world and its tangible results that we do not know where to look or how to see.

We need this new quality of consciousness in order to recognize and read the signs of God. Without the co-operation of His lovers, this new consciousness cannot be born, cannot be established in the collective. His lovers may look only to their Beloved, but they are also pledged to humanity, "slaves of the One and servants of the many." They are needed now to work together.

What does it mean to work together? It means to consciously recognize a purpose beyond one's individual path. Mystics do not proselytize, because they know that one of the greatest gifts of love is freedom. And yet we live in a world that has forgotten this freedom, this clarity of consciousness, this knowing born of devotion. Humanity has forgotten its place in the mandala of creation, in the great wholeness of life. It has lost its dignity, and instead of looking towards God, thinks only of material well-being.

His lovers are here to help redeem what has almost been lost. They have walked through the desolation of their own darkness and know the perils of corruption. They have been betrayed and ignored, isolated and made desperate. They know the hunger for what is Real because they live it. And they know the wonder of grace, the miracle of transformation through which He reveals Himself to Himself within the heart. And they need to work together to give humanity what it needs, what the soul of the world is crying for. It is no longer enough to work in isolation, to claim the inner secrets behind the closed doors of seclusion. While the path will always be walked in solitude, its meaning needs to be shared. His lovers need to create a collective affirmation of the ways of love, and of a consciousness that can recognize His hidden face.

The inner silence of love takes us beyond ourself, beyond every pattern, beyond every form. In this silence we are remade, reformed according to His will. We have experienced the seed of divine consciousness being placed within our own heart, and how it awakens us to the knowledge of His presence. As the eye of the heart opens, the mystery of Self-revelation takes place. He has said "We will show them our signs on the horizons and in themselves, until it is clear to them that He is the Real" (Qur'an, 41:53). What we have found within ourself we need to give to humanity—a new quality of consciousness to recognize the Reality that is always present around us, to realign us to the changing nature of His unchanging Self. Only then can humanity read His signs and come to know who we really are—once again see His face reflected in His world. It is for the mystic to make this new quality of consciousness accessible to herself and to humanity. This is the need of the time.

DIVINE MANIFESTATION

When we recognize the signs of God, the divine can manifest, can make itself known in a new way. Our conscious participation in this process is paramount. Consciousness is the catalyst for evolution, and a consciousness attuned to the signs of God has unknown potential. Consciousness is His gift to humanity, and when it is used in relationship to the higher frequency of the divine, the possibilities for our evolution are beyond our imaginings, because they belong to the hidden secret of life.

The idea that "what you think so you become" is based upon the relationship of consciousness to life experience. Serious spiritual students and "positive thinking" practitioners know that our inner attitude becomes reflected in our outer life. But we have little understanding of the possible effect of a consciousness that is aligned with the divine, that *consciously* gives space for Him to manifest His will. Only the lover who has surrendered to love, the wayfarer who has given herself to God, knows the miracle of His will enacting itself in her life. To experience His grace as a tangible reality is one of the wonders of the path. To be surrounded by divine providence that directly answers our need is to awaken to a quality of life that can hardly be imagined.

At present our collective consciousness is caught in a rational framework of cause and effect. We see life primarily from a temporal perspective. In the West we do not give divine providence its central place in our everyday activities. The divine has been pushed to one side of our frame of reference. In the midst of our frenzied activities we do not realize the effect of this attitude. We do not know how our stance of consciousness determines the whole of our life. More significant, we seem unaware that there are other attitudes of consciousness that can have very different effects, that can create a different experience of life. One of the aspects of Western hubris is to consider our present rational-material consciousness the only sensible way to live. Even in our sincere desire to redeem some of the problems our culture has created, we use the same approach that has, in essence, created the problems. And we remain remarkably unaware of the effect of banishing the divine from its central place in life and in our consciousness.

It is necessary and urgent to redeem this condition. Our consciousness is the vehicle for the divine to reveal itself in this world, for what is hidden to become manifest and known. If our collective consciousness can become re-attuned to the divine, the divine can become manifest. We are aware of the *absence* of the divine in our daily life, how collectively we are no longer nourished by the presence of the sacred. But our culture has no frame of reference to envisage the effect of divine *presence*. Part of the result of the patriarchal era was to banish God to the heavens and thus starve the material world of the sacred. What could be the effect of the divine returning to matter, of the heaven and earth uniting?

When we acknowledge the presence of the divine, its power and love have more direct access to our lives. The mystic knows this from her own experience. But until now this happens only to individual seekers, and is often at variance with the collective experience. What would happen if the divine manifested within the collective? If His presence became a normal part of our everyday life? What could be the effect of a collective consciousness that acknowledged His continual presence?

We tend to associate collective spirituality with imposed dogmas or ideas. But the lover knows that real spirituality is freedom, a freedom that embraces and yet is beyond every form. Ibn 'Arabî celebrates this when he writes the beautiful lines:

> My heart has become capable of every form:
> > it is a pasture for gazelles, and a convent for
> > > Christian monks,
> And a temple for idols, and the pilgrim's Ka'ba,
> > and the tables of the Tora and the book of the
> > > Qur'an.
> I follow the religion of Love: whatever way
> > Love's camels take, this is my religion and
> > > faith.[5]

Lovers live the freedom that belongs to the heart, in which every atom of creation is a manifestation of the divine mystery. This quality of consciousness is a seed within the heart of every human being, because we all carry the stamp of our Creator who is absolute love and freedom.

If this secret can be made known, if this potential of the human being can be made public, then the heart of the world can open and recognize that it is made in His image, that there is nothing other than God. For so long we have forgotten Him, abused Him and abandoned Him. Do we need to continue this collective misery, this alienation from our divine and human nature? Or can we look to a future born from the eternal present in which that which we love is no longer a hidden secret, but known and honored as the sacred substance of everyday life— the mystery of the divine made manifest? Then humanity can consciously play its part in the dance of the divine, in the celebration of His oneness.

When the heart of the world opens it is like spring returning after a long winter, like the song of one's first love becoming alive. The mystery and wonder of life are around us, no longer just a forgotten memory of childhood. We all long to recapture this eternal present, this completeness of our essential nature. But our culture points us down a different road, towards the gods of materialism and the demons of alienation. Do we dare to reclaim what belongs to us, to return to our first love? Or is our collective forgetfulness too painful to be faced?

What can be born is a state of being in which life is present in all the chaos and beauty of its contradictory qualities, joy and sadness, love and fear. But this dance of life is steeped with the presence of That which is the eternal substance of our own self, the oneness to which we belong. The light is all around us, and the darkness is permeated with the softness of a lover's touch, the fragrance of what is real. What we long for has already been given, if we would only recognize it. The signs of God are alive and are calling us by our real name.

Appendix
Learning to Read the Signs of God:
Dreamwork as a Spiritual Practice

Dreamwork is the modern equivalent of the ancient Sufi teaching stories.

Irina Tweedie

The ideas discussed in this book need to be lived, need to become a part of our everyday reality. Our consciousness has to change, to become attuned to the divine that is alive in every moment. Sufi dreamwork is an example of a spiritual pratice that teaches us how to awaken to this presence and learn to read the signs of God.

THE TRADITION OF SUFI DREAMWORK

The interpretation of dreams has always been an important part of the Sufi tradition. Early Sufi manuals have sections on dreams, which offer differentiation between "true" and "false" dreams, the latter being dreams without psychological or spiritual value. "True dreams" are those which offer guidance. Traditionally, dreams are interpreted by the *sheikh* or the representative of the *sheikh*. The twelfth-century Sufi, Najm al-dîn Kubrâ, stressed the importance of dreams and their interpretation, including in the rules of the path, along with "constant silence, constant retreat and constant recollection of God," "constant direction of a *sheikh* who explains the meaning of one's dreams and visions." In more recent times, in *Daughter of Fire*, Irina Tweedie gives a contemporary autobiographical account of a training with a Sufi master who regarded her dreams as offering important guidance. At the beginning of her training he told her, "Your dreams you must tell me and I will interpret them for you. Dreams are important. They are a guidance."[1] On his death in 1966 she returned to England, where she began a Naqshbandi meditation group. When I first came to the small room in North London where she lived, we would tell her our dreams or visions and she, or someone she asked, would interpret them. But over the years a change took place: the dreamwork evolved into a group process. Dreams would be shared and discussed within the group, people being encouraged to offer their own interpretation of a dream. Slowly group dreamwork became an important part of our meetings. We would meditate, have time for tea and talking together, and then we would share and discuss dreams. As the path spread and meditation groups formed without the physical presence of the teacher, this combination of meditation and dreamwork became the pattern of the meetings.

Sufism evolves according to the need of the time and the place and the people. Although the inner essence of the tradition can never change, the outer form adapts in response to the changing need. This is reflected in the development of dreamwork within this Naqshbandi tradition. Bahâ ad-dîn Naqshband, the founder of the order, was renowned as an interpreter of dreams. He also stressed the value of group discussion. In the words of Bahâ ad-dîn, "Ours is the way of group discussion." As this path has evolved in the West these two aspects of the Naqshbandi path have come together in the form of group dreamwork. Like many Sufi practices, spiritual dreamwork functions on different levels. It also has a purpose that is related to the need of the present time, the need to reclaim a symbolic and mystical consciousness.

GUIDANCE ON THE PATH

The Naqshbandi Sufi path has little outer form or structure. Apart from our basic practices of the meditation of the heart and the silent *dhikr*, we are rarely told what to do or given direct outer guidance. We learn to listen within, to the guidance that comes from the heart and from our dreams. Sharing a dream within the group, we affirm this inner guidance. Just in the simple sharing of a dream something is acknowledged and validated by others on the path. We also gradually learn about the wisdom of the dream, how it guides and directs us both inwardly and outwardly. We see how the hidden meaning of a dream can be understood, how its images and symbols can be interpreted both psychologically and spiritually.

The Naqshbandi path has always had a strong psychological element. Much of the work of purification is psychological, involving the confrontation with the shadow as well as other psychological processes. Dreamwork guides us through the maze of our own psyche, uncovering rejected and discarded aspects of ourself, revealing the light hidden in the darkness. Through our dreams we can also recover spiritual aspects of ourself that we misunderstood, for example a quality of devotion or service that has litttle echo in the outer world. Our dreams uncover both our light and our darkness, and often show us that the path is not as we expected.

Through sharing our dreams and listening to those of others we also learn to value the uniqueness of our own path, of our own way of journeying Home. We are each taken to God in our own way, according to the uniqueness of our individual nature. It is so easy to try to identify with others, to walk the path we see being lived by others. Others can inspire us, but we can only walk our own path, follow our own dream, live our own destiny. Our dreams tell *our* story, how the path unfolds within us. When we share a dream, the uniqueness of our own path is given attention. And through hearing the dreams of others we can see how for each of us the journey of the soul is different, demands different qualities.

Working with dreams, we learn to read the signposts on the way, to listen with an ear attuned to the music of the path, to the frequency of the soul. We uncover what we need to know, read the next step that we need to take. Sometimes we are shown a distant horizon—where this endless journey is taking us. But dreamwork is not just about interpretation, about finding out what the dream means. Dreamwork is a dialogue, a conversation between the dreamer and the world of the dream. Through this dialogue we make a connection to a part of ourself that the outer world often dismisses and invalidates. We reconnect with our dreaming, with the soul as it speaks to us in the ancient language of images and symbols. And when we share dreams in a meditation group this dialogue is heard by other people's hearts and validated within a sacred space. This is an important affirmation of the dream, and of the soul that speaks to us through our dreams.

If you believe in your dream it will attract the interpretation, the response it needs. The Jungian Werner

Engel said, "The dream will always make itself known." A dream is a living, dynamic reality that attracts the attention it needs. The interpretation may not be perfect; it may even be wrong. You may not discover the real meaning of a dream until weeks or even years later. Dreamwork is not about right or wrong, but a process through which we work with the world of the psyche. Through dreamwork the energy of the inner world is made accessible to us. Through trying to understand our dream we participate with the inner world, and its energy can come into consciousness, come into our waking life. We are nourished by our dreams more than we know, and dreamwork helps us to access this nourishment, be fed by the *manna* of our dreamworld.

REESTABLISHING A SYMBOLIC CONSCIOUSNESS

Through working with dreams, listening to their symbols and images, trying to understand their meaning, all those present are participating in an important work, that of reestabishing a symbolic consciousness. There was a time when mankind's primary mode of thinking was symbolic, and all of life was understood as rich in symbolic meaning. We have lost that way of thinking, buried it deep within us. As a result we are no longer nourished by the meaningfulness of our daily lives: for example, the ordinary activities of hearth and home, cooking and nurturing, no longer carry a symbolic meaning—we no longer honor these gods.

Symbolic consciousness makes all of life holy; all of life becomes an interaction with the divine. The rituals of life nourish us more than we can imagine, because they reconnect us with the deep roots of our being and with the whole of which we are a part. With the advent of rationalism in the West we slowly banished symbolic consciousness and lost touch with our inner heritage. Time became just a succession of hours and days, rather than a part of the great round in which the seasons follow the constellations. We have recently become aware of how civilization has alienated us from the outer world of nature; we have little awareness of how we have been cut off from our inner nature.

There are many aspects of life which can only be understood symbolically, for example our transitions through the stages of life, the "seven ages of man." Without a symbolic understanding we are confronted primarily with the physical effects of aging, and do not have access to the deepening awareness of our own nature that comes through these different initiations into life and then what is beyond life. Without being nourished by a world of symbols, we are left increasingly stranded in a materialistic world that does not reflect our deeper nature. Hungry for symbolic meaning, we often try to find symbols in our outer life—we look for the gods on our television screen, we glorify our car or computer. We work harder and harder in search of our goals, but something essential is missing, and we feel a poverty even if we cannot name it.

Our culture's alienation from the symbolic world has caused many problems, particularly for women. The nature of the feminine is more in tune with nature and the symbolic world; and more than the masculine she needs to be nourished by the symbolic—the cycles in her body have a ritual rather than rational quality. Trying to understand the feminine rationally has sadly distorted and disempowered her: her nature is crying out to be honored symbolically.

Rituals cannot be imposed, nor can we create our own symbols. Symbols and rituals belong to life and evolve from an interaction with the inner world. They are a gift from the gods. Our rational Western culture is the only culture that has tried to evolve without a conscious interaction with the inner world, and we appear to have reached the limits of this experiment. There is a primal need to reconnect with the archetypal and symbolic world, to reclaim the images of the soul. As Helen Luke writes, "Only the images by which we live can bring transformation.... Each of us has a well of images within, which are the saving reality and from which may be born the individual myth carrying the meaning of life."[2]

But in order to access this world of images we need to reclaim this quality of consciousness, this ancient mode of thinking. Symbolic consciousness belongs to the right side of the brain and is holistic rather than the left brain's analytic mode. The left hemisphere is equated with logic and thinking in words, and develops with the acquisition of language. It is fundamentally directed towards the outside world. The right brain is more directed towards the inner world. Rather than thinking in words it thinks in images, and, as opposed to the active, idea-forming process of the rational mode, is primarily receptive, observing the change and development of its images.

Symbolic consciousness, also known as "matriarchal consciousness," allows for the formation of symbols and so for a symbolic relationship to life. Symbolic consciousness also allows for wholeness and harmony, which according to the Native American, Chief Luther Standing Bear, is the essence of civilization and the true fostering of our humanity:

> The man who sat on the ground in front of his tipi meditating on life and its meaning, accepting the kinship of all creatures and acknowledging unity with the universe of things, was infusing into his

being the true essence of civilization. And when native man left off this form of development, his humanization was retarded in growth.[3]

But in our Western world symbolic consciousness has been repressed by the increasing dominance of analytical, directed thinking. Symbolic thinking has been devalued, and for the majority it exists unrecognized in the unconscious, expressing itself only in dreams, fantasies, and vague feelings. That symbolic thinking can be so suppressed has recently been corroborated by the neurological discovery that the left hemisphere can repress or inhibit the activities, and especially the emotionally toned activities, of the right hemisphere.[4] Interestingly, women do not have such a clear distinction between the activities of the left and right brain, which means that in women symbolic consciousness cannot be so easily repressed.

If we are to live in harmony with our deepest nature, we must reclaim this holistic mode of thinking. Through dreamwork we are reaffirming this forgotten language, this quality of consciousness. Meeting as a group week after week, year after year, listening, appreciating, talking in the language of symbols, we validate something that has been rejected and denied. We open a door to the symbolic world, a door that can then remain open not just for ourself but for others.

Dreamwork takes place at the threshold between the inner and outer worlds. As a Sufi group we work in the inner world and in the place where the inner and outer world meet. Dreamwork opens a door between them in ourself and also within the consciousness of the group. And because the inner world is not limited by the same space-time considerations that exist in the physical world,[5] the door within the group consciousness can become an open door within the larger sphere of the collective. What we affirm as a group we affirm within the collective and the door that we open can be accessed by others.

Symbolic consciousness opens the door for a symbolic relationship to life and to our deeper nature. It allows us to have access to the inner figures of wisdom and power, the wise old man or woman, the child with stars in her eyes, who inhabit our dreams and from whom we can learn the wisdom of our soul. Yet there are no books to teach us how to access these images, to remind us of these skills of communication. Dreambooks may tell us about the meaning of certain symbols, but one cannot learn a language just from a dictionary. Like anything that has been repressed, this language lies buried within us, waiting to be rediscovered. We have to find our own mode of inner listening through which we can awaken this ancient understanding.

Listening to dreams for a few hours a week, we can regain the art of being receptive, of listening with an ear attuned to love and to the hidden meaning of the symbolic world. The importance of the feminine quality of receptivity has been forgotten in our masculine world. In the words of Helen Luke:

> It is exceedingly hard for us to realize, in the climate of Western society, that the woman who quietly responds with intense interest and love to people, to ideas, and to things, is as deeply and truly creative as the one who always seeks to lead, to act, to achieve. The feminine qualities of receptivity, of nurturing in silence and secrecy are (whether in man or woman) as essential to creation as the masculine opposites and in no way inferior.[6]

Dreamwork can help us to reclaim the feminine art of listening, the creative quality of receptivity, and can open to us a doorway into the symbolic reality of the soul. When we listen to a dream we not only hear the words but visualize its images. We enter the temple of the imagination and participate in its mystery of a symbolic universe.

We also learn to listen to the subtleties of feelings and emotion. This is important if we are to make conscious our relationship to both our inner life and the archetypal world that is its foundation. Carl Jung clearly stated that the archetypal world only becomes alive and meaningful through its feeling and subjective affect:

> Those who do not realize the special feeling tone of the archetype end with nothing more than a jumble of mythological concepts, which can be strung together to show that everything means anything—or nothing at all. Archetypes come to life only when one patiently tries to discover why and in what fashion they are meaningful to a living individual.[7]

Through being receptive to the feelings evoked by a dream, we find our way into a diffuse world that is rich in undefined qualities and archetypal resonances. What had seemed like a backwater of our inner self we discover to be teeming with life, full of the wondrous and unexpected.

Dreamwork in a group also teaches us to listen without judgment or criticism, or the preconceptions that easily color our conscious life. We learn to be attentive, alert, and responsive to the needs of others. When a dream is told we put ourself to one side and attune ourself to another's journey, to her struggles, confusions, and joys. We see how the path works for others, that what is easy for one person is difficult for another. And deeper than our differences we share the same search, the one journey of the soul going back to God.

THE UNION OF MASCULINE AND FEMININE THINKING

Practicing dreamwork we listen and respond to the deeper meaning of the dream, appreciating its symbolic reality. Through the work of discussion and interpretation we also attempt to make conscious the meaning of the dream. Some elements of a dream can not be interpreted, but should remain within the mystery of the dream: if they are interpreted they lose their magical quality, their ability to express the mysteries of the soul. But many aspects of a dream need to be interpreted, need to have their significance understood, in order for the dreamer to be guided by their images and enriched by their wisdom. However, in working with a dream we always need to be aware that the dream comes from a reality that is deeper and older than that of rational consciousness. We must bring an attitude of respect to the dream, knowing that although we may consciously interpret a dream it will always point us beyond the boundaries of our rational consciousness, nourish us with what is unknown.

Dreamwork requires an attitude of receptivity and attention in which we learn to first listen and appreciate the wisdom of a symbolic world, and only then use our analytic mind as a tool of dream interpretation. Our masculine, analytic mode of thinking can help us to understand more fully, more consciously, the purpose and meaning of our inner self, grasp the guidance it is offering us. But our masculine thinking must be in service to the feminine inner world and its symbolic mode of expression. We cannot allow our rational mind to follow the patriarchal pattern of attacking or dismissing the wisdom and knowing of the feminine. The delicate fabric of a dream can only too easily be torn apart by an analytic approach that does not respect its subtleties, its feeling qualities and ambiguities. Then the meaning and wisdom of a dream become lost to consciousness, and we remain separate from our symbolic self. Dreamwork necessitates that we reclaim a masculine mode of thinking that is in harmony with rather than antagonistic to the feminine.

The masculine which honors the feminine lives in our psyche.[8] This is a quality of the masculine that belongs to our higher nature, to our inner nobility. It can reflect on the symbolic richness of our inner nature, value individual feelings and the relatedness of life, and yet also carry the clear light of detachment and discrimination. This masculine respects the darkness, appreciating the mystery and beauty of the feminine, and how her instinctual knowing embraces the wholeness of inner and outer life. The inner masculine also offers us an attitude of consciousness through which we can live in harmony with our inner self, and come to recognize the clarity of the feminine through which the sacredness of life is made known. Together with the feminine, this masculine can help us to catch the thread of our higher nature, and so guide and direct us.

Working with dreams both individually and as a group we can reestablish a balance between masculine and feminine consciousness that allows them to work together, and thus bring about a union of masculine and feminine, of analytic and symbolic consciousness, through which a deeper and richer understanding of our real nature can become part of our consciousness. We can come to appreciate how we are a part of a interrelated whole in which our inner self nourishes and guides us.

CATCHING THE DIVINE HINT

Working with dreams, we gradually become familiar with a reality that is not fixed or static. Dreams are amorphous and changing, and their meaning is neither logical nor pre-determined. Responding to dreams, we have to catch their meaning as it belongs to the moment, a moment that is outside of time and outside of the defined parameters of our rational mind. Dreamwork thus helps us to listen and be responsive to a different, more fluid dimension, and can prepare us for the difficult work of catching the divine hint.

The aim of the spiritual training is to lead a guided life, guided by that within which is eternal. The divine often guides us through hints, which we have to catch and respond to without rational understanding. This is the way of Khidr, the Sufi archetypal figure of direct revelation, a direct and unconditional inner connection with the divine. In the story of Khidr told in the Qur'an, Moses, who represents the established law, wants to follow Khidr and be guided by him. But Khidr tells him, "You will not be able to bear with me. For how can you bear with that which is beyond your knowledge?" (Qur'an 18:61-62).

Walking the mystical path of love, we are taken into a reality we cannot understand, which is beyond our preconditioned knowledge. We have to learn to listen and respond from a place of unknowing—to be an empty cup. This is a very different attitude from that demanded by the outer world, which requires that we act from a place of knowing and understanding. Dreamwork can help to awaken the part of our brain that can respond without preconceptions.

In the outer world we learn to build upon a basis of knowledge. For example, once you know what a tree is you know this for the rest of your life. You may build upon your initial knowledge of a tree and come to know more about a tree, or about different types of trees. But each piece of knowledge remains, and often the more you know the more you are valued in the world. This a static mode of thinking, which is based on the accumulation of knowledge.

Working with a dream, we learn to put our preconceptions to one side, to be an empty and receptive space in which the wisdom and meaning of a dream can make itself known. While an understanding of symbolism can be helpful, this is always secondary to the initial experience of the dream in which we listen for the dream to reveal itself, to tell us its story. The dream comes from a deeper and wiser part of ourself than our conscious mind. Therefore the primary attitude we need in approaching a dream is that the dream knows something we do not. We stay in a place of unknowing as we allow the dream to reveal its meaning.

Through dreamwork we learn to work with not-knowing. We see what happens, what can be revealed, when we allow ourself to be unknowing. This is very different from our mental conditioning. But it is a good training for the mystical path which also requires us to have the attitude that we do not know either where we are going or how to get there—"only the lost are found." The mind does not have any understanding of the real mystical process because it takes place beyond the mental level. In the words of the Sufi master Bhai Sahib, "What can be understood by the mind is not a high state." Mystical reality is based upon not-knowing, upon emptiness.

In dreamwork we interact with a reality that is less fixed and more dynamic than the outer world or our rational mind. Listening to dreams, we attune ourself to this fluid inner world in which things are rarely as they appear. As images shift and change, so their meaning evolves; so hidden parts of the dreamer become known. Gradually our consciousness becomes adapted to functioning in this non-linear, more dynamic mode.

Working with dreams, we leave behind the fixed world which is familiar to the rational mind, and to which, through our education and upbringing, we have become conditioned. Instead we consciously participate in a constantly changing reality which we cannot rationally understand. Dreamwork trains the mind not to be caught in any fixed image or idea, and not to judge or have any preconditioned response. There is also a humor in dreams that laughs at our preconceptions or dissolves our established sense of self. Dreamwork frees our consciousness from the rigidity of any imposed pattern, and can awaken us to the laughter and freedom of our true self. It can prepare our consciousness for the work of catching the divine hint.

The divine hint is "quicker than lightning" and if we interfere, through any judgment or censorship, the hint is lost. If we respond, "What if...,' or "But...," or "I am not sure...," or any of the mind's conditioned responses, then the hint is lost, the opportunity gone. A divine hint requires that we listen and act accordingly. Nor will a divine hint always be about an action. Sometimes it is something we need to know, a quality we need to develop, an attitude we need to change. What matters is that we are always attentive and respond in the moment. We do not weigh up the consequences or consider our actions. We listen and act. But in order to listen and respond unconditionally, the mind has to become free of many patterns of conditioning. We have to leave behind our normal desire to understand, to know what we are doing. Dreamwork can help to free our mind, to enable it to work at this higher, faster level.

Through dreamwork we learn to work with what is at the borders of consciousness, what is undefined, what has not yet come into being. The mind learns to catch hidden subtleties, nuances of meaning, and to respond to the need of the moment. Through dreamwork we also develop our intuitional consciousness—suddenly you just understand the meaning of a dream, you "get it." There is no linear progression of understanding that leads to this knowledge. Suddenly you know something. Intuitional consciousness is an aspect of the consciousness of the Higher Self, and is very helpful in learning to catch the divine hint which belongs only to the moment and does not originate in one's own thinking process.

Dreamwork is a stepping stone to catching the divine hint. But it is not the same as catching the hint. Dreamwork is a process through which we uncover the meaning of a dream. The hint is just given, and the only participation of the wayfarer is to listen and then respond. The hint works at a much higher vibration than dreamwork. But through dreamwork we can realign our consciousness and work with our mind in a different, non-linear way. Individually and as a group we work at the threshold of consciousness, at the borders of the unknown. We tune into what has not yet taken form, rather than what is already fixed and defined. Dreamwork trains us to listen to the voice of our Beloved, to be attentive to Him.

THE GOLDEN THREAD

Spiritual dreams are those that come from the soul. They teach us about symbols and the meaning that is hidden under the surface. They guide us through the labyrinth of our psyche and tell us about our real destiny. These dreams help us to uncover the real nature of our being, to recognize its quality and bring it into our everyday life. They have within them a "golden thread" that is the destiny of the soul, our own direct connection to God.

Spiritual dreams are an elaboration of this "golden thread," giving it the coloring and texture of the moment, of the time and the place and the people. Working with these dreams, we align ourself with this innermost quality, this sense of Self. We become alive to this ancient and eternal part of our being. Through dreamwork we become nourished by the numinous and by our own connection to what is sacred and eternal. First we glimpse this thread, and then learn to recognize it. Gradually it becomes the path that we follow, the guidance we need. We learn to know this thread as the unique nature of our spiritual life, of our whole life.

This golden thread cannot be recognized with our rational mind, but our symbolic consciousness sees it, and the consciousness of the heart knows its purpose. Through working with this thread, seeing how it is woven into our dreams and hidden within our daily life, we discover that it belongs to the foundation of both our inner and outer life. This thread *is* our deeper self living within us, giving color and substance to the images of our psyche and also the texture of our days.

The practice of dreamwork in a spiritual group makes us aware of how this thread is present in the dreams and lives of others. We see how easy it is to overlook, and how it often appears in a form we do not think of as spiritual, even overlook as insignificant. Many times it is present as an image or event in a dream that seems to be out of place with the rest of the dream. Because the destiny of the soul is so different from the agenda of our ego-self, even our "spiritual" ego-self, this thread will be found where we least expect it. Our "golden thread" is always leading us beyond our preconceptions, into a state of unconditioned freedom.

Through the hearing and discussion of the dreams of others, as well as in our own dreamwork, we discover this thread and see how it affects our outer life. We learn to see how this deeper destiny is woven into our everyday life, how outer situations and events have this hidden essence. We learn to recognize this quality of the divine not just in meditation or moments of ecstasy, but in the midst of life. And as we see it within our own self and within our life, we carry this consciousness for the whole. Both individually and as a group we support what is essential to life, and to life's making its deeper meaning known. In this way we validate what the world does not validate, we affirm what the world has forgotten.

This "golden thread" belongs to the essence of love and the way love comes into the world. It is a connection between our life and the love that is the foundation of life, and it carries the consciousness of love. It is one of the ways His love has access to the world. Recognizing and following this thread, we follow the way of love, see how the texture of His love is woven in our life and in the world.

To become conscious of this thread of love is an important contribution to a world that has fogotten this primal mystery. The "golden thread" of the soul, the thread of His love, is hardly known of today, is rarely written about. His lovers belong to love and have the eyes of love, the awakened eye of the heart through which this mystery is made known. They are working to make this wisdom accessible so that once again we can be guided by love, live according to the ways of the soul.

Seeing this thread within our self, recognizing it in the dreams of others, we are bringing this knowing into the collective thought-form of our time. Individually and together we are working to reestablish a quality of consciousness that is based upon the direct connection of the soul to God. This connection is always present, but when we make it a part of our consciousness, then the miraculous can become manifest.

We do not appreciate the power of consciousness, in particular the potential of a consciousness aligned to the divine. When we recognize the signs of God, the connection between the human and the divine resonates, and a frequency of love is given to humanity. With each age the effect of this frequency changes, according to the evolutionary potential of humankind. Without this frequency, this knowledge of love, there can be no transformation. Humankind will remain in the present state of stagnation. But if we become aligned to our true nature, then our deeper destiny can become part of our outer life, not just remain an inner dream. If the knowledge of love and the ways of love becomes accessible to those who need, the work of the mystic has been done. Then those who love the world for His sake can turn their faces to their Beloved knowing that His gift has been brought into the marketplace of the world, that His song can be heard in the hearts of all those who need Him. In a new way the golden thread of His destiny for His world will sing with the celebration of His divine nature. His name will be known again within the heart of the world and the consciousness of His people.

Notes

LOVER AND BELOVED

1. Quoted by Sara Sviri, *The Taste of Hidden Things*, p. 9.
2. Nizamî, *Layla and Majnun*, p. 195.

LIVING THE MOMENT OF THE SOUL

1. Trans. Coleman Barks, *Say I am You*, p. 62.
2. "Burnt Norton" ll. 34-39, *Four Quartets*.
3. "Tintern Abbey" ll. 95-98.
4. "Who gets up early to discover the moment light began," *Those Branching Moments*, trans. John Moyne and Coleman Barks.

THE POWER OF FORGETFULNESS

1. *The Secret Rose Garden*, trans. Florence Lederer.
2. I have written extensively on the importance of a spiritual group in *In the Company of Friends*, especially pp. 8-16.
3. The symbol of the Great Mother, Ouroboros, the serpent eating its tail, images the closed circle of the unconscious that does not allow the development of individual consciousness.
4. T.S. Eliot, "Burnt Norton," ll. 168-175, *Four Quartets*.
5. Quoted by R.S. Bhatnagar, *Dimensions of Classical Sufi Thought*, p. 58.
6. Rûmî, trans. Andrew Harvey, *Light upon Light*, p. 79.

EFFORT AND GRACE

1. Irina Tweedie, *Daughter of Fire*, p. 404.
2. Tweedie, p. 58.
3. Tweedie, pp. 536-537.
4. Tweedie, p. 134.
5. Najm al-dîn Kubrâ, quoted by Henry Corbin, *The Man of Light*, p. 72.
6. Rûmî, quoted by Chittick, *The Sufi Path of Love*, p. 198.
7. Rûmî, translated by Coleman Barks, *Feeling the Shoulder of the Lion*, p. 61.
8. Rûmî, quoted by R.A. Nicholson, *Mystics of Islam*, p. 113.

COMPLETENESS

1. Tweedie, p. 451.

RECOGNIZING THE SIGNS OF GOD

1. Trans. Coleman Barks, "The Bright Core of Failure," *The Glance*, p. 89.
2. *Hadîth*, quoted by William Chittick, *The Sufi Path of Knowledge*, p. 103.
3. Quoted by Stephen Hirtenstein, *The Unlimited Mercifier: The Spiritual Life and Thought of Ibn 'Arabî*, p. 157.
4. "The Burial of the Dead" ll. 19-24.
5. Quoted by Hirtenstein, *The Unlimited Mercifier: The Spiritual Life and Thought of Ibn 'Arabî*, p. 203.

APPENDIX

1. Irina Tweedie, *Daughter of Fire*, p. 12.
2. "The Perennial Feminine," *The Way of Woman*, p. 15.
3. Quoted by T.C. McLuhan, *Touch the Earth*, p. 99.
4. A. Stevens, *Archetypes*, p. 265. The two hemispheres of the brain are joined by the *corpus callosum* which is a bundle of nerve fibres. It is via the *corpus callosum* that the left hemisphere can repress or inhibit the right hemisphere.
5. Which is why, for example, dreams can sometimes be prophetic.
6. "The Perennial Feminine," *The Way of Woman*, p. 15.
7. C.G. Jung, *Man and His Symbols*, p. 96
8. In our Western culture this was imaged by the knights of courtly love who were always in service to "Our Lady."

Bibliography

Bhatnagar, R.S. *Dimensions of Classical Sufi Thought.* Delhi: Motilal Banarsidass, 1984.

Chittick, William C. *The Sufi Path of Love.* Albany: State University of New York Press, 1983.

—. *The Sufi Path of Knowledge.* Albany: State University of New York Press, 1989.

Corbin, Henry. *The Man of Light in Iranian Sufism.* London: Shambhala Publications, 1978.

Eliot, T.S. *Four Quartets.* London: Faber and Faber, 1944.

—. *Collected Poems.* London: Faber and Faber, 1963.

Jung, C.G. ed. *Man and His Symbols.* London: Aldus Books, 1964.

Harvey, Andrew. *Light Upon Light.* Berkeley: North Atlantic Books, 1996

Hirtenstein, Stephen. *The Unlimited Mercifier.* Ashland, Oregon: White Cloud Press, 1999.

Luke, Helen. *The Way of Woman.* New York: Doubleday, 1995.

McLuhan, T.C. *Touch the Earth.* London: Garnstone Press, 1972.

Nicholson, R.A. *Studies in Islamic Mysticism.* Cambridge: Cambridge University Press, 1921.

—. *The Mystics of Islam.* London: Arkana, 1989.

Nizamî. *The Story of Layla & Majnun.* Trans. R. Gelpke. London: Bruno Cassirer, 1966.

Rûmî. *Those Branching Moments.* Trans. John Moyne and Coleman Barks. Providence, Copper Beach Press, 1988.

—. *Feeling the Shoulder of the Lion.* Trans. Coleman Barks. Putney, Vermont: Threshold Books, 1991.

—. *Say I am You*. Trans. Coleman Barks. Athens, GA: Maypop Books, 1994.

—. *The Glance*. Trans. Coleman Barks. New York: Penguin, 1999.

Shabistarî. *The Secret Rose Garden*. Trans. Florence Lederer. Grand Rapids: Michigan: Phanes Press, 1987.

Stevens, A. *Archetypes*. London: Routledge & Kegan Ltd., 1982.

Sviri, Sara. *The Taste of Hidden Things*. Inverness: Golden Sufi Center, 1997.

Tweedie, Irina. *Daughter of Fire: A Diary of a Spiritual Training with a Sufi Master*. Inverness, California: Golden Sufi Center, 1986.

Vaughan-Lee, Llewellyn. *In the Company of Friends: Dreamwork in a Sufi Group*. Inverness, California: Golden Sufi Center, 1994.

Wordsworth, William. *Poetical Works*. London: Oxford University Press, 1936.

Index

A

Abû Sa'îd ibn Abî-l Khayr
(d. 1049), 13, 38
adolescence, 26
America, 53, 65
archetype, archetypal, 54,
56-58, 112, 115, 118,
127
attention, 14, 15, 18, 24,
28, 51, 56, 59, 67, 72,
73, 75, 84, 86, 89,
90, 92, 100, 109, 110,
116
awakening of the heart, 18

B

Bahâ ad-dîn Naqshband
(d. 1390), 107
Bâyezîd Bistâmî (d. 874), 60
Bhai Sahib (d. 1966), 35, 63,
71n, 72n, 88-89, 119

C

chaos, 77, 82, 83, 105
Christ, 42
Christianity, 30
conditioning, 22, 23, 24, 25,
26, 32, 53, 54, 56, 60,
61, 78, 84, 87, 98, 120
collective conditioning,
34, 53, 65
mental conditioning,
119

rational conditioning,
85
Confederate, 67
consciousness, 12, 13, 19, 20,
29-32, 44, 48, 52, 69,
71, 73, 75, 78, 79, 83,
87, 106, 110, 112, 113,
117, 120-125
changes of conscious-
ness, 90
collective consciousness,
24, 31, 43, 91, 102, 103
consciousness of love,
52, 123
consciousness of the
heart, 88, 122
divine consciousness,
12, 34, 71, 96, 98, 101
intuitional conscious-
ness, 121
masculine consciousness,
96
matriarchal conscious-
ness, 112
mystical consciousness,
58, 78, 99, 108
patriarchal conscious-
ness, 48
rational consciousness,
77, 78, 86, 87, 116
symbolic consciousness,
110-114, 117, 122
courtly love, 127

Acknowledgments

For permission to use copyrighted material, the author gratefully wishes to acknowledge: Andrew Harvey and North Atlantic Books, for permission to quote from *Light Upon Light: Inspirations from Rumi* by Andrew Harvey (1996); Maypop Books, for permission to quote from *Say I am You* translations of Rûmî by Coleman Barks (1994); Shambhala Publications, for permission to quote from *Feeling the Shoulder of the Lion* translations of Rûmî by Coleman Barks (1991); Copper Beach Press, for permission to quote from *Those Branching Moments* translations of Rûmî by Coleman Barks and John Moyne (1998); White Cloud Press, for permission to quote from *The Unlimited Mercifier: The Spiritual Life and Thought of Ibn 'Arabî* by Stephen Hirtenstein (1999).

LLEWELLYN VAUGHAN-LEE, Ph.D., has followed the Naqshbandi Sufi Path since he was nineteen. In 1991 he moved from London to northern California, where he now lives with his family. He lectures throughout the United States and Europe.

THE GOLDEN SUFI CENTER is a California Religious Non-Profit Corporation dedicated to making the teachings of the Naqshbandi Sufi Path available to all seekers. For further information about the activities of the Center and Llewellyn Vaughan-Lee's lectures, please contact us at:

The Golden Sufi Center
P.O. Box 428
Inverness, California 94937

tel: (415) 663-8773
fax: (415) 663-9128
e-mail: goldensufi@aol.com
website: http://www.goldensufi.org

OTHER TITLES PUBLISHED BY
THE GOLDEN SUFI CENTER

BY IRINA TWEEDIE

DAUGHTER OF FIRE
A Diary of a Spiritual Training with a Sufi Master

BY LLEWELLYN VAUGHAN-LEE

THE BOND WITH THE BELOVED
The Mystical Relationship of the Lover and the Beloved

IN THE COMPANY OF FRIENDS
Dreamwork within a Sufi Group

TRAVELLING THE PATH OF LOVE
Sayings of Sufi Masters

SUFISM, THE TRANSFORMATION OF THE HEART

THE PARADOXES OF LOVE

THE FACE BEFORE I WAS BORN
A Spiritual Autobiography

CATCHING THE THREAD
Sufism, Dreamwork & Jungian Psychology

THE CIRCLE OF LOVE

LOVE IS A FIRE
The Sufi's Mystical Journey Home

BY SARA SVIRI

THE TASTE OF HIDDEN THINGS
Images of the Sufi Path

BY PETER KINGSLEY

IN THE DARK PLACES OF WISDOM

A selection of live talks given by Irina Tweedie, Llewellyn Vaughan-Lee, Sara Sviri, and Peter Kingsley are available. Further information is available through our website or contact us for a free catalog.